GET IT TOGETHER!

GET IT TOGETHER!

AN INTERIOR DESIGNER'S GUIDE TO CREATING YOUR BEST LIFE

ORLANDO SORIA

PHOTOGRAPHS BY **ZEKE RUELAS**

PRESTEL

MUNICH + LONDON + NEW YORK

© Prestel Verlag, Munich · London · New York 2018
A member of Verlagsgruppe Random House GmbH
Neumarkter Strasse 28 · 81673 Munich

Prestel Publishing Ltd.
14-17 Wells Street
London W1T 3PD

Prestel Publishing
900 Broadway, Suite 603
New York, NY 10003

Library of Congress Cataloging-in-Publication Data

Names: Soria, Orlando, author.
Title: Get it together! : an interior designer's guide to creating your best
  life / Orlando Soria ; photographs by Zeke Ruelas.
Description: New York : Prestel Publishing, 2018. | Includes index.
Identifiers: LCCN 2017033796 | ISBN 9783791383705 (hardcover)
Subjects: LCSH: Interior decoration. | Self-realization.
Classification: LCC NK2115 .S614 2017 | DDC 747—dc23
LC record available at https://lccn.loc.gov/2017033796

A CIP catalogue record for this book is available from the British Library.

Editorial direction: Holly La Due
Design and layout: Amy Sly
Production management: Luke Chase
Copyediting: John Son
Proofreading: Kelli Rae Patton
Index: Kathleen Preciado

Verlagsgruppe Random House FSC® N001967

Printed in China
Second printing 2018

ISBN: 978-3-7913-8370-5

www.prestel.com

FOR MY BOYFRIEND. JUST KIDDING I DON'T HAVE ONE.

CONTENTS

9 Introduction

CHAPTER 1 / INTERIOR DESIGN FUNDAMENTALS

14 When You Have a Gay Midlife Crisis

22 What to Do with That TV Money

30 Let's Face It, You Need a Beach House

38 Creating a Home That Is Inviting Yet Intimidating

46 When You Realize You're Losing Your Mind So You Move to Suburbia

54 When You Design Your Dream Home with Your Boyfriend Then He Dumps You

63 When You Finally Get Your Own Place After Living with Roommates Forever

CHAPTER 2 / DESIGN TIPS-N-TRICKS

74 Picking a Wall Color That Won't Make You Barf

82 Hanging Art Sucks Let's Do It Together

88 Selecting a Rug That's Not a Huge Bitch

94 Intergenerational Relationships: Mixing and Matching Vintage and New

100 Common Rookie Mistakes to Avoid

104 Down in the Dumps: Creating a Post-Breakup Space Where Your Life Can Stop Sucking

110 Creating a Space That Reflects Your Awful Personality

115 If Your Kids Are Brats It's Probably Your Fault for Not Making Their Rooms Cute Enough

122 Crisis of Masculinity: Designing for Dudes

CHAPTER 3 / HOMME LIFE

132 How to Make Non-Garbagey Flower Arrangements

135 How to Throw a Major Rager

142 What You Need in Your Dumb Kitchen

146 How to Throw a Dinner Party for Like No Money

152 Begrudgingly Hosting a Guest

158 How to Be Your Own Maid

162 Plant Your Rage in a Container Garden

CHAPTER 4 / LIFE ADVICE

170 Living with a Roommate or Boyfriend Is Terrible

174 What to Do When All Your Friends Have Babies at Once

178 What to Do When You Randomly Gain 50 Pounds

182 How to Deal with a Soul-Sucking Breakup

188 What to Do When You've Been Laid Off and Your Life Is Ruined Forever

193 I Hate Your Wedding

196 Do You Hate Your Friends?

CHAPTER 5 / DO IT YOURSELF

202 How to Make Your Own Orblando Out of Hardware Store Garbage

206 Make Your Own Goddamn Coffee Table

211 A Basic Tray to Impress Your Friends Who Are Also Basic

216 I'm Ashamed of This Shitty DIY

220 A Side Piece For Your Sofa

224 Making a Wooden Bench as Simple as Your Mom

228 Life Is Meaningless Let's Make a Swing Shelf

232 Conclusion

234 Acknowledgments

235 Index

INTRODUCTION

OK, so this is going to be hard for both of us. I have to write something to explain what this book is about and you have to read it. Actually, I guess you don't have to read it but something in your life, some awful mistake or terrible bit of karma, brought you to this point where you are reading this very word and you don't have the strength to peel your eyes away. Rather than take your destiny into your own hands, you're just going to passively keep reading and for that I'm thankful.

LOOK INTO MY EYES.

Remember when you were little, like right before the school holiday program, being totally nervous about playing Santa and fucking up your lines? You were like, "THIS IS MY ONE CHANCE TO PROVE TO EVERYONE HOW AMAZING I AM." That's kind of how I feel about this book. I've always wanted to write a book. AND NOW I'M DOING IT AND YOU'RE READING IT! So many important things are happening right now! THIS IS MAJOR. Let's be honest, I'm probably going to fuck it up. But you'll never know how royally I ruin this opportunity if you don't keep reading. Don't you want to watch me fail? Keep reading!

Hey lady, guess what?!? You just read two paragraphs and literally nothing happened! I'm sorry, I was nervous. I should have been telling you what you can expect from this book! That's what happens in a normal introduction. But this is not a normal introduction. I'm going to take you all the way back to my birth to explain why I am the only person you should listen to when it comes to home decor, life issues, and DIY projects. LITERALLY THROW ALL YOUR OTHER BOOKS INTO THE DUMPSTER.

My love for home life began the second I was born. In a house! Unlike most of the cold, clinical people you know, I was born in a warm, cozy house. Literally. It was the '80s and the home-birth movement was having a major moment. And my formerly BerkeleyPeople parents decided to have us at home. So literally the first thing I saw when I came into the world was a house. Which is why I'm so much better at interior design than everyone else. Sorry, I know

that sounds pompous, but I have to convince you of my prowess, otherwise why on earth would you keep reading this book?

After my parents had their three kids at home, they did something even more insane. They moved us all to the middle of the woods. I grew up deep within Yosemite National Park, literally feet away from the Lower Yosemite Falls. This insanely idyllic upbringing may have lacked the shopping malls and urban amenities I wanted as an awful teenager, but it was the perfect place to spend hours alone making things and thinking about design. By the time I was seven I'd redecorated my bedroom like a million times and made just about every kind of craft you can possibly imagine.

Most of my childhood was spent looking out my window at Yosemite Falls (seriously), reading *The Andy Warhol Diaries*, plotting my escape to New York, and screaming things like, "SOMEDAY I'M GONNA GET OUT OF HERE AND THEN YOU'LL ALL BE SORRY!" I'm gonna leave the rest of my life story out because I'm already getting bored. But let's cut to the reason I named this book *Get It Together!* I'm going to explain this in three easy steps.

GET YOUR INTERIORS TOGETHER

One, Get It Together! refers to what you'd expect it to refer to if you have any idea who I am or what I do. For those of you who don't know (who are you and what are you doing here?), I'm an INTERNATIONALLY RENOWNED INTERIOR DESIGNER TO THE STARS. I wrote that as joke, but it's kind of true. There are random people around the world who know who I am AND I have done a lot of work with celebrities. That just kind of happened and I'm not going to take credit or responsibility for it. But yeah, I'm kind of a big deal and you should listen to everything I say as if it were written on a piece of paper that was dyed with tea and its edges burned so it looks like an old pirate map. The contents of this book are THAT important.

Get It Together! is a call to action for women and men of all ages. It's a statement that says, "LET'S TAKE YOUR HOUSE FROM FLAB TO FAB IN LESS THAN SIX MINUTES, YOU DUMB WHORE!" The main reason I stick with interior design (rather than becoming a famous fashion model or actor, despite constant requests to do so) is that creating a beautiful living space is a way to show care for yourself and care for others. It's a way of saying to yourself, "I'm worth more than this pile of empty tuna cans with a beach towel on it that I'm using as a sofa!"

What I'm saying is that it's time you stopped living like a stupid college kid and started investing in your space. I have a crazy aunt who lived somewhere for three years without buying furniture. I was like, "AUNTIE LINDA YOU NEED SIDE TABLES," and she was like, "BUT I DON'T KNOW WHAT TO BUY!" Here's my advice: if you don't know what to buy, just buy something cheap/vintage and replace it later when you realize how ugly it is. You gotta rip off the Band-Aid otherwise you're going to be sleeping on the floor forever. NO MA'AM NOT ON MY WATCH. GET IT TOGETHER!

GET IT TOGETHER AND DO IT YOURSELF

Another fun way to Get It Together? By making stuff yourself, DUH! As I explained a bit before, I started making things myself at a very young age because I lived in the middle of the woods and had like no friends. While this sounds sad and lame and boring, it ultimately ended up benefiting me because now I'm better than everyone else at making stuff. Except when I'm not (read on: there's a major FAIL in this book that is sure to delight you. LAUGHING AT THE MISTAKES OF OTHERS IS FUN!). Do you think Martha Stewart became the queen of DIY by being well-liked and popular? NO WAY. I'm sure there were some moments of her crying alone as a child, making things out of papier-mâché in the woods, before she became queen of everything. GREATNESS IS BUILT NOT BORN PEOPLE.

Making things on your own might sound like a waste of time (and money) but it's not. It's a way of understanding your own abilities. And also a way of surrounding yourself with things you really value. Think about it: if there's a pretty lamp in a room, are you going to like it more if you bought it or more if you made it? The power that comes with knowing your own creative abilities is invaluable to your self-esteem. Knowing you can make things with your hands shows you that when the End of Timez comes, you'll be able to craft your own boat to navigate the rising waters. AND WHAT'S MORE FUN THAN THAT?

Got a pile of garbage you wanna make into a bowl? Get It Together! and DIY until your hands bleed! I'll show you how.

GET IT TOGETHER AND LISTEN TO ME

Ever notice how therapists are always the biggest messes on earth? I think it's scientifically proven that people who work as therapists have way more personal problems than everyone else. This is why I'm the perfect person to help you figure out how to deal with your totally fucked-up life. Need to know how to act at the wedding of someone you hate? I got you! Need to know what to do when the love of your life dumps you? I'm here for you.

I've learned a lot of tricks to Get It Together! in my own life, and I'm here to share those strategies with you. Mostly, getting it together is about coming to peace with things and realizing that you have no control over most things. And the things you do have control over might not be worth controlling. So what we'll talk about in this book is how to deal with life's challenges without losing your mind (unless losing your mind is called for).

So please, come closer, I need to whisper something in your ear. Are you close yet? I'm gonna cup my hand to your ear and murmur something into it:

GET YOUR LIFE TOGETHER!
BUT FIRST, A WARNING

NOW A WARNING?!? You guys, we're about to embark upon the most important journey in all of our lives, especially yours. But first, a few caveats about what you're about to get yourself into.

I wrote this book from the depths of a pretty deep depression. I'm telling you this not to make you feel sad or worried (by the time you read this my life will be awesome; I'll be in Capri with my new gorgeous Italian boyfriend, drinking Lambrusco and throwing euros into the sea for fun, I guarantee it). I'm telling you this because we all go through terrible times. And it is my belief that acknowledging how terrible they are while trekking through them is the only way to get through. If you are suffering and your life sucks right now, know that what you're going through is only temporary. That was literally exactly where I was as I typed these words. AND MAYBE EVEN WRITE A STUPID BOOK ONE DAY!

In this midst of writing this book, my life fell apart. I lost my boyfriend, my job, and my apartment in the course of just a few months (literally in the middle of the photo shoots and writing for this book). Well, I guess I didn't actually *lose* those things: my boyfriend *dumped* me, my job *dropped* me, and the dream condo I'd designed with my boyfriend *was no longer mine*. I was devastated and heartbroken and lost and life didn't seem exciting or worthwhile anymore. What was left to be hopeful about? It was an incredibly painful time and literally everything was awful. I moved in with my parents for a few months to finish this book, get some peace and quiet, and, quite frankly, because after losing my job, boyfriend, and apartment all at once, I was reeling financially.

How could this happen to someone so far into his career? I'd been working for years in my field, but multiple setbacks at once can send anyone for a loop. I wasn't prepared to deal with so many setbacks at once. And that's why I got megadepressed while writing this book.

BUT DON'T BE SAD YOU GUYS! I have an uplifting point, I promise!

Life gets shitty. And some of the best workarounds for the resulting depression lie within this book. Firstly, refreshing a space, making something yourself, or taking a moment to laugh or improve yourself are the best things that can come from a life trauma, whether that be the loss of someone you love, the loss of a job, the loss of your home, or anything else that comes your way. Fixating on making things beautiful can be a great way to ensure you don't fixate on THE OVERWHELMING DARK THOUGHTS THAT LIVE DEEP WITHIN YOU.

Sometimes the only way we can get through things is to laugh our fucking heads off. Which is why you'll notice that the tone of this book is light and frivolous. I'm hoping that if you bought this book you came here to have fun. For years, interior design has been written about in such dry, formulaic ways. It's time that we started having fun with it. As my friend Emily Henderson used to say, "If we screw this up, no one's gonna die" (unless of course you designed a chandelier out of swords and it fell down and decapitated everyone at a fancy dinner party, that would suck). What we're talking about here isn't that precious. We have to be willing to laugh about it, to play with it, and to make mistakes. People who are freaked out about making mistakes probably won't make any. But they probably also won't do anything cool or worthwhile. The point of this book is to stop taking yourself so seriously and start doing shit. Life is too short to live in an ugly house, too scared to buy anything or make it yourself. Get It Together!

The reason there's even a client base for me as an interior designer is that most people are too scared to make any decisions themselves because they're afraid of making the wrong choice. I'm here to tell you, EVERYTHING YOU'VE HEARD ABOUT DESIGN RULES IS A LIE. There are some rules, but there are exceptions to every single rule. So if someone ever gives you concrete rules about interior design, life, or DIY, know that they are lying in an attempt to manipulate and control you. If you encounter one of these people, start yelling gibberish into their face until they run away.

So yeah, that's my intro. In this book I'm gonna give you the goss on how to Get It Together! And quite honestly, if I can write a book from the depths of one of the lowest depressions I've ever had (which will be gone by the time you read this because I've published a book which is obviously the funnest thing I've ever done) then you can take on any project that lies within these pages.

I believe in you. No more excuses. Now is the time to GET IT TOGETHER!

INTERIOR DESIGN FUNDAMENTALS

What's a chair? And why won't it stop yelling at you and chasing you around the house? Do chairs always have eyes and mouths like that? Wait, was that a breath mint you just took or a tab of acid? These are questions we all find ourselves asking from time to time. And that's why I'm here! This chapter is all about the fundamentals of interior design and style. Here, we'll tour a variety of gorgeous homes and talk about the dos and don'ts of interior design. We'll also chat about how design can help you deal with all the awful situations life throws your way. How can you design an apartment with your boyfriend quickly, before he dumps you? When is it time to escape the city and head on out to the suburbs? What should you do if your gay face is getting old and gross? The answers to these and other important questions await you! Come on in!

WHEN YOU HAVE A GAY MIDLIFE CRISIS

WHAT IS A GAY?

For those of you who may not have met one, a Gay is a man like no other. His skin is supple and cocoa-colored, regardless of his race. His teeth are pearly white, like a gleaming moon on a romantic July night. His hair is perfect and alluring. It moves naturally when wind hits it, but it always returns to a natural, gorgeous man-coif once the wind has subsided. A Gay's laugh is infectious, echoing violently through a room, causing everyone to stand at attention, a shocking tingle running down their spine as their posture tightens (they know they could be the object of derision at any moment).

Gays tend to move in packs of six or more, usually wearing short-shorts, neon tank tops, and expensive sandals that make them look like Greek warriors. Their hair is filled with natural-looking highlights that cost more than my car. Gays make great companions as they are cleaner, funnier, and better house-trained than gross straight guys. But beware of the Fashion Gay, who will wait until you leave the room to say something so cutting about you that if you heard it you would be shattered forever.

Gays like many activities, including dancing, laughing, and repeating quippy one-liners like "YAZ KWAYNE" to groups of befuddled straight people. In fact, gays love dancing so much that if you put on a tune they'll start dancing involuntarily (it's in their DNA!). Gays love dancing on floats, they love dancing on boats, and they love dancing on goats. Just kidding about the goat thing. But it *did* rhyme. Speaking of goats, scientists agree that if gays are allowed to marry, pretty soon we'll all be marrying goats. IS THAT THE KIND OF LIFE YOU WANT FOR YOUR CHILDREN?

WHEN DOES A GAY KNOW HE'S OLD?

There comes a time in any man's life when he wakes up, looks in the mirror, and realizes he is old and gross. For a Gay, this is age twenty-six, when he enters into Gay Middle Age. Gay Middle Age is when the sparkle disappears from a Gay's eyes, he realizes he now has to hide in a sleeping bag in the linen closet until he dies because no one will ever love him. It's a difficult time for a Gay. However, different Gays respond to aging with different coping mechanisms. Some Gays get plastic surgery until their faces look like cats. Some Gays buy youthful boyfriends on the Internet and go around wearing age-inappropriate clothes such a shell necklaces and asymmetrically cropped mesh tank tops.

A Gay knows he's old when his best girlfriend goes out dancing with a younger version of him. "Sorry, James," she'll say, "Ceth listens to cooler music than you and still looks like a wax figurine." Being Gay is like being a magical, fragile flower. For a time, you are the most beautiful, delicate thing on earth. And the next day you're garbage. NEXT!

HOW TO DESIGN A YOUNG SPACE TO DISTRACT FROM YOUR GROSS DISGUSTING OLD FACE

As they begin to age, a Gay will do his best to slowly divert your attention from his former go-go-boy body to the decor around you. You too can follow along with these homosexual tricks as your face slowly begins to rot off your skull! Remember this simple formula: for every 10 percent grosser your face and body get, make your home

10 percent more beautiful. The loveliness of your home will counterbalance how revolting you've become and quickly distract your guests from your Apple Doll face.* You see, Gays have known for centuries the secrets I am imparting to you here. Make your house gorgeous so no one will notice you look like the contents of a sarcophagus.

*IN CASE YOU DON'T KNOW WHAT AN APPLE DOLL IS, IT'S A DOLL WHOSE FACE IS MADE OUT OF AN APPLE THAT'S LITERALLY DRIED UP AND ROTTEN. I USED TO SEE THEM AT CRAFT FAIRS ALL THE TIME WHEN I WAS LITTLE AND THEY SCARED THE SHIT OUT OF ME.

AS COLOR FADES FROM YOUR HAIR, ADD IT TO YOUR DECOR

As a Gay ages, he needs to compensate for the color disappearing from his hair by adding color to his decor. This is why when you go to an older Gay's home it's mostly just bright drapes and fluffy pillows and mannequins dressed in original '80s Madonna costumes. Gays are good at color, so be sure to take note of how they use it next time one invites you into his home. For some reason, Gays have superior eyeballs and can create better color combos than all other humans. Moms agree, Gays know what they're doing when it comes to color!

ACTUAL TIPS FROM A REAL GAY

MIX SHAPES / Gays know that diversity is key to creating a space that looks better than everyone else's. That's why they're not scared to add sculptural elements to their homes. Why does a pillow need to be a square? LET'S TRY A CIRCULAR PILLOW! Need something to plop onto the dining table? TRY A STARBURST. There doesn't need to be a reason for something to be a fun shape. A Gay knows that a diversity of shapes makes a home A HOME.

SIGNS OF GAY AGING

1. Crow's feet
2. Overuse of gay youth slang (i.e., YASSS HUNTY)
3. An overwhelming desire to go to Coachella
4. Shirtless selfies at Burning Man
5. Playing circuit party* music at dinner parties
6. Cat face
7. Laser hair removal
8. White BMW convertible
9. Inappropriate scarves
10. Small dogs
11. Black-and-white male nudes as home decor
12. Talking too much about CrossFit

*A circuit party is a shirtless dance party with restricted access available only to Gays with 2 percent body fat or less. The music is usually terrible and basic.

USE PINK / A little-known fact about Gays is that in the privacy of their own homes they wear nothing but pink satin ball gowns, fancy high heels, and gold necklaces with charms that read "DID SOMEBODY SAY WINE?" It's been downplayed by the Hollywood liberal elite media, but it's true. Gays know the power of pink. It's important to balance the masculine and feminine energy in a home. So, if you have a masculine beige sofa, why not use your limp Gay wrists to throw some pink pillows on it!

MIX ERAS OF FURNITURE / While Aged Gays are shunned by their community, Gays do love Aged Furniture.

Adding in a vintage chair or side table to contemporary furnishings will make you look smart, sophisticated, and superior to everyone you know. Furnishings with some age bring character and historic presence to a space.

FIND A HOT PIECE OF BRASS / Gays love brass. Adding brass accents to your home helps diversify finishes, which in turn helps makes your home look collected and cool. This glamorous bedroom (previous spread) gets a little kick from brass accents on the bed and nightstands. The brass finish provides warmth and a reflective surface to bounce light onto your gross aging face.

YOU MUST HAVE DRAPES! / Nothing pisses off a Gay more than a house without window treatments. Inviting a Gay over to a naked-windowed home is considered a hate crime in forty-eight states and can cause irreparable harm to a Gay's emotional well-being. Even if you're not worried about privacy or light protection, adding window treatments finishes off a room and makes it feel complete and considered. Don't let your windows go naked, this is not a beach in Europe!

PRACTICE PARTICULARITY WITH PATTERN! / As with all of life, working with patterns is a smart time to choose your battles wisely. Gays know you can't have patterns everywhere. You have to choose where to go patterned and where to keep it simple so your eyes don't have a panic attack. Like you and me, eyeballs need a place to rest. If you have patterns all over the place, your eyes will get fatigued, causing you to slowly lose your mind. For example, in this Gay's home—which was designed by my friend Matthew Lanphier—the floor is a gorgeous multicolored tile pattern so you'll notice there's not a lot of pattern elsewhere. Gays know you have to let a star be a STAR.

WHAT TO DO WITH THAT TV MONEY

SAY GOODBYE TO YOUR DREAMS, THIS IS L.A.

Hollywood. It's the place where dreams come to die and where dreamers come to do drugs at rich people's houses. It's the place where one minute you're IN, and the next you can't even get a job at In-N-Out Burger. It's the place where you can be top billing at the box office one week, and the next you get top billing as one of those people who spins signs on the corner when it's 150 degrees outside. It's the place where one day you look like a gorgeous, supple green grape, the next you look like a shriveled-up raisin someone left to bake in the sun during a nuclear apocalypse. It's the land of dreams all right. The type of dreams a haunted porcelain doll has after her face has shattered in half and she's been left in the attic for a hundred years and spiders are crawling into her eyeballs. BUT HEY, THE WEATHER IS GREAT!

There's a reason that old beggar woman who lives in my apartment (oh wait, that's me!) says "YOU'RE NEVER GONNA MAKE IT IN THIS TOWN" to passersby. This town seems like it's all pools, candy, and gay boys in teeny bikinis. But it's really the most cutthroat place on the planet. Not only do you have to be wealthy, successful, and gorgeous, you have to do all of it while pretending it's easy and literally never going to work. Think about it, have you ever seen an Angeleno go to work? Not a single one of us has a real job. Sometimes I'll go to the gym at noon and, surrounded by models, actors, and gay men with cat faces, have a nervous breakdown and scream out loud, "WHY AREN'T ANY OF YOU DICKS AT WORK??? Does anyone in this town have a job???"

No, no, they don't.

And that's how I know that L.A. is the land of the undead. None of us need money or jobs because we long ago sold our souls to the devil in exchange for semiannual trips to Palm Springs and regular access to a pool. But it's cool, because pools are totally refreshing! Seriously though, I have no idea what most people in L.A. do. But I do know for a fact that none of them work. That's why there's an average of fifteen cafés for every one Los Angeles resident; and 100 percent of the people at said cafés drink 47 percent of the world's rosé at any given time. I've always been curious what these people do for a living that they can drink rose at 11 a.m. on a Tuesday, but now I know. They don't have jobs, their moms are sending them rent money, and they're taking some sort of secret diet pill that keeps them from getting obese from drinking all that rosé. I haven't found out what the pill is but as soon as I do I'll be one of these rosé guzzlers, too.

ADDING CONTEMPORARY ACCENTS TO A MID-CENTURY HOME

One thing Angelenos love is plastic surgery and transformation. Which brings me to this house! It was originally a mid-century two-story home. But with the help of a fantastic architect (The Los Angeles Design Group), the owner transformed it into this majestic manse. The issue with the old house was that it had very small windows with structural apron-awnings that hung over the windows, making the whole place feel dark and terrifying, like a dungeon filled with angry ghosts. As with most L.A. makeovers, the goal with this project was to give the space a lift and make it brighter, tighter, and more youthful.

With a contemporary home, minimalism is normally the go-to style for decorating and furnishing. But that doesn't mean the home has to be a total snoozefest. We added colorful tile, sculptural light fixtures, and a number of structural accents to this place to make it appeal to the eclectic taste of its owner, a Hollywood insider who will stop at nothing to get what he wants. I even traveled all the way to Barcelona, my new favorite city on earth, to seek out an extra special light fixture for the stairway. Designed by the creative team Goula / Figuera, this light fixture adds an extra sense of POW to the home. As an added bonus, it's not yet sold in the United States, so my client is the only one who has it. And in L.A., the only thing better than owning something trendy is owning something that literally no one else has. CAN YOUR DESIGNER DO THAT?

1. Coke coffee table (self-explanatory)

2. Windows with city views (from which you can look down on other people)

3. Guest bedrooms for when your guests accidentally Quaalude themselves into a coma but you're too drunk to take them to the hospital but also don't want to call an ambulance because REPUTATION

4. A sofa wide enough for at least six Hollywood egos

5. A painting of a man who may or may not be Morgan Freeman

6. Vintage accessories from the Rose Bowl Flea Market you paid someone to go find for you

7. Telescope to remind your guests they're not the only stars in the room

8. Round mirrors (these belong in literally every home)

9. Statement bathrooms (this is the only room in the house where people will stop performing long enough to notice their surroundings)

10. Modern lighting (to remind everyone that you're cooler than them)

FITTING A DINING ROOM INTO A MULTIFUNCTIONAL SPACE

The trademark of most Hollywood Hills homes is a multifunctional room with a kitchen, dining room, and living space combined. This is important when you have people over for parties because they like to fantasize about cooking even though most of them haven't used their own arms and hands to cook anything since they left the farm in Louisiana (sidenote: everyone who lives in L.A. is from a farm in Louisiana). Having a multipurpose space tells your guests, "I'm just like you (but better)," and it also serves the most important function of all, making sure the refrigerator full of Veuve is never too far away.

STARS, THEY'RE JUST LIKE US (BUT BETTER!)

How do we pull off this Hollywood look without dipping into our trust funds or having to sacrifice our monthly face-lifts? Well, this look is pretty simple to pull off, as long as you remember a few key Tips-N-Tricks!

1. IN A CONTEMPORARY SPACE, WHITE SHOULD BE THE GO-TO DEFAULT FOR WALL COLOR. This is because most contemporary spaces tend to have fewer decorative moldings than traditional spaces. In ye olden days, basically every architectural detail had a border around it. Now, doorframes, windows, floors, and ceilings exist without molding—there's no natural stop for a paint color. SO IF YOU PAINTED ONE ROOM BLUE THE WHOLE HOME WOULD HAVE TO BE BLUE AND THAT WOULD BE COMPLETELY BONKERS. This and the fact that most contemporary spaces get lots of natural light (if it doesn't, MOVE OUT!) make white the best default.

2. CHOOSE A LIGHT AND LUMINOUS FINISH FOR YOUR FLOOR. No dark, shiny flooring in here! Instead, choose a mid-to-light tone wood to echo the bright, happy sentiments of the white walls.

3. MIX AND MIX AND MIX! Hollywood may have a diversity problem, but that doesn't mean your house has to! Mixing materials (wood, leather, lacquer, mirror, metals, stone, etc.) gives your modern space a subtle earthiness that contrasts with the space's inherent sterility.

4. ADD VINTAGE. Yes, I've said this elsewhere in this book and I'll say it again until I myself am vintage. Adding vintage (like this amazing sofa) gives your space a sense of age and history. It's like the difference between planting a sapling and planting a four-hundred-year-old tree. Duh! The four-hundred-year-old tree is gonna be way more interesting. Put a new tree and an old-ass tree next to each other. You'll def wanna hug the old-ass tree a lot harder than that stupid teeny baby tree. FUCK YOU BABY TREE!

5. MINIMAL DOESN'T HAVE TO MEAN BORING. While it's important to keep minimal spaces free from too much clutter or from looking overly "designed," small hints of individuality are important. For example, the Hollywood tycoon that owns this place made his own paintings that we added to his bedroom. Their handmade look keeps the space from looking too generic and boring.

6. CIRCULAR ART TELLS YOUR FRIENDS YOU'RE NOT SQUARE. I love incorporating unconventionally shaped artwork into my projects. Especially projects that are as edgy and as cool as this Hollywood abode. This simple painting (following page) adds some visual softness to the room along with some handmade flava.

7. SHARE YOUR HOBBIES! Your home's decor should hint at your hobbies (unless your hobbies are creepy and gross). Adding in accents like a telescope helps make a space feel like your own. Telescopes are also an excellent accent because they provide the decorative height that normally only a plant can provide. But they won't die when you leave them to go to Cannes for the film festival then take an extra few weeks to hang out in the south of France (which, DUH, you have to, it's amazing there!).

HOW TO SURVIVE A
HOLLYWOOD PARTY

You might not be able to tell from looking at me, but I've been invited to a few Hollywood parties in my day. I know what you're thinking. BUT, GRANDMA, HE'S SO OLD. But I wasn't always an old Apple Doll Lady. I've attended many a fancy Hollywood party, and learned many important lessons from doing so. Here are a few Tips-N-Tricks I'll share with you!

1. Be ten hours late and you'll still be a half-hour early. I don't know how this works; it just does. This is why whenever I invite Hollywood elites to my parties I tell them they're happening twelve hours before they actually start. This way they'll only be two hours late. Being late makes a Hollywood person feel important, so expect them to be so late the party is over, you've cleaned up the whole mess, and started another party. Those monsters will be *that* late!

2. If you don't know anyone, just go up to a random person and be like, "Hey! It's me, [insert your name]! We worked together on Jenji's show!" This will trap them into talking to you for hours. They'll feel guilty for not knowing who you are and have no idea whether or not you are powerful enough to get them booked on next season's most important TV show.

3. Drink until you slur your speech. Then drink some more. No one will judge you and they'll actually find it refreshing that someone was "real" enough to not sit there fake-sipping on booze while networking like a creep. You'll become known as the fun one. People will just point in your direction and be like "That's Barb! She's the fun one!"

4. If you run out of things to talk about and your captive friend seems like she might escape, seductively whisper one of the following three phrases: "Integratron," "Moon Juice," or "Ojai Valley Inn and Spa."

5. If you have kids, don't mention them. No one cares that Little Timmy is finally potty trained. They are here to forget about their boring everyday lives. AND YOURS.

6. If someone asks where your cheap-ass fast-fashion outfit is from, say "It's Kelsei." As if that were a real brand. They'll be too embarrassed to admit they don't know what Kelsei is. And they'll think you're totally rich and glamorous.

LET'S FACE IT, YOU NEED A BEACH HOUSE

YOUR LIFE SUCKS

Something we need to establish before we can continue is how truly awful your life is. You wake up, eat a depressing breakfast, struggle through the traffic gridlock of whatever city you live in to get to work, work all day at a job you hate for a boss that's a total asshole, and then go home to stare at the wall and think about how you never thought life would be like this. I get it. I once was where you are now. I once was part of the rat race. Thankfully, for most of my adult life I have been unemployed, struggling my way out of abject poverty. Yes, it was annoying that I couldn't afford all the Mary Kate and Ashley Olsen for Marc by Marc Jacobs backpacks I wanted, but I don't have a boss. And the only person I have to answer to is myself. And my mom, whom I live with, as an adult human male.

EVERY DAY IS WORSE THAN THE LAST

Remember graduating from college when you were like, "THE WORLD IS MY OYSTER!" And then like two years later you were all "DOES ANYONE HAVE ANY METH?" It's not your fault. Life is hard because we have to work and working is boring. You know what's fun? NOT WORKING! Working normally means you have to sit at a stupid ol' desk and do stuff for other people. Like answering emails. And then when you answer those emails people just send you EVEN MORE EMAILS. Modern times have made us all into postal workers. Remember the '90s when all those postal workers went berserk because THE LETTERS JUST KEPT COMING AND COMING AND COMING? Well, now we have that but with emails and WE ALL HAVE IT. It's only a matter of time before we all lose our fucking minds.

This is why I have over twenty thousand unread emails as I write this. I tried to keep up but too many people kept reaching out so eventually I just gave up. Someday I'm hoping to be rich enough to hire an underling to go through all of them. Or just delete them all at once. Until then, I'm just pretending they don't exist. The point is that our lives are terrible and we are bound by all these dumb-ass tasks that we hate doing but we all keep doing anyway because we don't know what else to do because we're scared if we stop doing them we'll be left behind forever when the next technological advance comes.

IF YOU DON'T GET OUT OF THIS GODDAMN CITY, YOUR HEAD WILL IMPLODE

The only way to deal with how absolutely monotonous life has become is to buy a beach house. Trust me, I've looked through all the other options and this is the only workable one. I don't know how you'll get your grubby little hands on a gorgeous, spacious house that overlooks the Pacific Ocean, but if you were resourceful enough to find this book and intelligent enough to have read this far, I trust you're resourceful enough to get the keys to a beach house. Apparently squatters have lots of rights in California. So if you can't afford to buy a beach house, try renting one in my home state and then refusing to leave! EVERYONE WINS! Except everyone that isn't you.

My dream is that someday I'll have my own TV show. I've actually been on TV before and I don't really like it all that much, to be honest. But my dream is that an old man who lives in Texas will see me on the TV show, buy me on the Internet, and force me to come and live with him in his giant southern estate. I'll stay at home learning to play the

piano and arranging flowers every day for the lavish dinner parties we'd throw every evening for local dignitaries. Then, one day he'd die and I'd sell the southern estate and finally move to Marin County, where my giant mansion would overlook San Francisco Bay and the Golden Gate Bridge. Of course, even though I lived in a home overlooking water, I'd also need a weekend house in Big Sur. So I'd use the rest of my inheritance to buy an enormous wood-shingled mid-century mansion on the Big Sur coast. PROBLEM SOLVED!

See? I figured out how to get a house overlooking the Pacific Ocean. SO CAN YOU! It might take a while. P.S. if you're an old man living in Texas and you're interested in buying me off the Internet, please contact the publishers of this book who can coordinate that purchase for you at your earliest convenience.

YOU MARRIED AN OLD DUDE, HE DIED, YOU HAVE YOUR BEACH HOUSE. NOW WHAT?

This is where it gets fun. Designing a beach house is like designing a regular house but way more enjoyable. Mainly because you don't have to live there all the time so if you fuck up you don't have to look at it all the time. The following are some tips on how to design the beach house of your dreams.

DON'T BE BASIC

The main thing to keep in mind when designing a beach house is not to be a total idiot. Don't put up signs that say shit like, "The Beach Is That Way" with an arrow pointing to the beach. Duh, we know that. We just walked in the goddamn door. FROM THE BEACH.

ADD SUBTLE HINTS OF BEACHINESS

While it's important to avoid accessories that are too on-the-nose, that doesn't mean you need to avoid all things beachy. You can add coastal hints by using materials and finishes that echo the textures and colors of the coast. By adding in items that subtly hint at the beach, you provide subconscious reminders for your guests that you have a beach house and they don't. For example, sisal rugs remind people of the color of sand. So when they see your sisal rug, they'll be reminded there is sand right outside your house and therefore you are better than they are.

BRING IN BLUE, DUH

By adding in subtle blue hues that hint at the luscious, blue waters of the ocean, you'll give yourself a gentle reminder that at any moment you could be swallowed up in the ocean's waters as global warming causes waters to rise dramatically. Beachy!

BEIGE IS NOT ONLY OK, IT'S ENCOURAGED

Beige has seen a major backlash in the past ten years, mainly because of its ubiquity in the '90s. But it is my belief that it's going to make a comeback, perhaps even before this book is published. Beach houses have always been the one place it's been OK to use beige. Soft, sandy colors like beige are always welcome in a bright, inviting beach house.

DID SOMEBODY SAY WHICKER?

Wicker doesn't have an "H" in it, but if you have it at your beach house make sure to refer to it as "WHICKER," overpronouncing the "H" as much as possible. This will make those around you feel as though they have entered a special time. A time before the Internet and email was invented. A time in which people didn't know how the fuck to pronounce "wicker." Oh, and the point of this tip is to add wicker. It's cute and adds a casual, vintage vibe to a beach house. Just don't let anyone sit on it if they're wet. In fact, if they look like they're about to sit down, shriek in their direction, "NOT ON MY WHICKER!!!"

DUH, NAUTICAL STRIPES!

If you don't like nautical stripes you have no reason to continue reading this book. JUST KIDDING KEEP READING PLEASE DON'T LEAVE ME! The classic navy-and-white stripes are a quick way to add a beachy feel to any space. Nothing makes people happier than seeing a preppy nautical stripe at a beach house. If you like JOY and FREEDOM, make sure to include some nautical stripes in your beach house's decor.

HANG A CREEPY LADY PAINTING ABOVE YOUR BED!

People might think you've gone soft by getting a beach house. Remind them you're still edgy and cool and might do heroin at any moment by putting a drawing of someone who may or may not be a satanic witch above your bed. Adding one-of-kind art is a great way to make your space feel sophisticated rather than generically beachy.

ADDING ART ON A BUDGET

We wanted to go high impact in the living room (previous spread) without spending too much. So I sourced some gorgeous wallpaper from Black Crow Studios and framed it. The result is the look of a giant custom-made watercolor painting at A FRACTION OF THE PRICE. Pretty sure I deserve a Nobel Peace Prize for this.

SHELL(F) STYLING 101

OK, so one of the elements I love most about this beach house is the gorgeous built-in shelving in the library/playroom/occasional guest room. The only problem? STYLING SHELVES IS A PAIN IN THE ASS. Here's why: YOU NEED A SHIT-TON OF BOOKS AND ACCESSORIES TO DO IT RIGHT. Here are a few tips I have for making sure your shelf styling comes out perfectly:

1. Think of the number of books you'd like to see on your shelving. Multiply that by eight thousand. Then make sure you have that many books.

2. You'll also need a considerable amount of accessories in small, medium, and large sizes. The way I like to source these is by starting at flea markets and thrift stores, seeking out treasures that have some age and history to

them. Then I like to go to big-box stores and buy A TON of other accessories with the understanding I'll return whatever I don't use. Buy twice to three times as much as you think you'd realistically be able to fit. The goal here is to make sure you have everything you need before you start styling your shelves so you're not standing there like a fool with an inadequate amount of props and no way to make it work.

3. Adding art onto shelving is a great way to break the monotony of books and objects and to add color. I like to use small-scale works (make sure they fit into the vertical space between shelves).

4. Once I'm styling, I work in the following order: books, art, large objects, medium objects, then small objects. Start by distributing books equally around the shelving, then add in art. I like to start in by adding the biggest objects first because that way I can balance things out with the medium and smaller objects. Usually it's best to have some items overlap and leave some breathing room between others. Generally, this is done by grouping things in odd-numbered groups of 3–5, but this is not a steadfast rule. I'VE SAID IT BEFORE AND I'LL SAY IT AGAIN AND AGAIN UNTIL MY CHEEKS EXPLODE OFF MY FACE, THERE ARE NO RULES IN DESIGN. This is why it's important to give yourself ample time to style your shelves. You're going to want to give yourself time to style your shelves because you're gonna need some time to step back and ask yourself, AM I DOING THIS WRONG?

CREATING A HOME THAT IS INVITING YET INTIMIDATING

PEOPLE ALWAYS ASK ME...

I'm often approached by major news outlets and leading journalists to give tips on how to be MORE CLASSY LESS TRASHY. I don't know how it happened, but I've always been held up as an example of class, elegance, and grace. One time, as a young child, I was at afternoon tea with Jacqueline Kennedy Onassis, and as we nibbled upon petits fours, a team of paparazzi screamed, "JACKIE! CAN YOU SCOOT OVER? YOU LOOK LIKE A GARBAGE PERSON NEXT TO ORLANDO BECAUSE HE IS SO ELEGANT!" Knowing she was outclassed, Jackie immediately left the table and was never seen at tea again.

You see, the one thing I learned growing up in a national park is how to be poised, perfect, and superior at all times. This comes in incredibly handy in my work as an interior designer, where I have to explain to people daily that their furniture, their homes, and their very souls are trashy and disgusting and need to be replaced with better, more expensive ones. Oh, you didn't know? That's what interior designers do. If it weren't for us, you'd all be running around like a bunch of bag ladies wearing flour sacks for dresses and thinking your reclaimed wood/Edison bulb light fixture was still cool.

If you are reading this, I know it can only be for one reason. You are the epitome of class, elegance, and grace. Otherwise how would you have come across me, purveyor of everything you need to know. I'm basically Gwyneth Paltrow.

Speaking of Gwyneth, I met her once and she is just as perfect and gorgeous as you'd think. Also, she doesn't let people wear shoes in her house, which made me like her even more because shoes inside is gross if you think about it. Like think about all the things you step on outside then think about all the times you put your face directly onto the rug. Also, her post-breakup relationship with Chris Martin (whose voice literally sounds like an angel and nearly caused me to faint when I met him briefly) is better than any relationship you've ever had. So basically Gwyneth's divorce is better than your marriage. DEAL WITH IT!

I'm not entirely sure why I brought her up except I feel like it's great goss and it's something I've never been able to share before for professional reasons. (I was at her house for a meeting about a collab I was doing with Goop.) And because classy, elegant people like me are very discreet and don't care about celebrities. Anyway, Gwyneth Paltrow is graceful and perfect AND YOU CAN BE TOO—if you listen to everything I say in this chapter VERY carefully.

THEY'RE MY GUESTS, WHY SHOULD I SCARE THEM?

The moment guests enter your home, their friend hats come off and their judging goggles come on. This means that while you were just laughing and joking a minute ago as you were walking in the door, now it's time for business. And that business is them entering your home, scanning the space for flaws, and quickly assessing your value as a human being. Their hawklike flaw-finding skills will immediately hone in on anything that is imperfect or un-classy. Their computer-like brains will record each offense and tabulate a score of your worth as a human being. This data will be shared directly with your entire network of friends.

I'm not sure how you became friends with such terrible, judgmental people, but don't blame me. In fact, who

your friends are is probably the result of many decisions YOU made. So I cannot be blamed for what judgmental assholes they are. Maybe it's time you looked in the mirror and thought about getting some new friends (see Chapter 4 for tips on how to tell if you hate your friends). If swapping out your friends for better ones sounds too hard, then the only alternative you have is to make your house so goddamn fancy that their judging goggles won't be able to spot any flaws.

That's how you're going to win. That's how you are going to beat them all AND BE THE BEST YOU CAN BE.

CAN I FEEL AT HOME IN A HOME THAT IS SO PERFECT?

Whenever I visit my parents—when I'm not living with them—I spend half the time yelling at them about how they

don't need that many things on their kitchen counter. At my house, I like to hide everything utilitarian from sight. Like coffee grinders, pans, food processors. In her kitchen, my mom's all "I use this every day, I'm just gonna put it on the counter next to the stove!" This fills me with uncontrollable rage. If you have the energy to use something every day, you have the energy to hide it from view when it's not in use. Leaving things on the counter is a reminder to your guests that you are a human being with human needs. AND NO ONE WANTS TO KNOW ABOUT THAT.

As you can imagine, being my family member is as terrifying as it is thrilling, never knowing when I could be like, "WHY IS THIS SPOON COLLECTION ON DISPLAY!?!" Because I am so elegant and classy, I like to constantly stand behind people making micro-aggressions about the state of their interiors. By the time I leave, their homes are always much more gorgeous than when I arrived. Part

of their souls may be gone, but the sacrifice is worth it because they will finally have the gorgeous home I always wanted them to have but they were too selfish to give me. I mean themselves.

BUT SERIOUSLY AM I CRAZY?

OK, so obviously it's not healthy to try to make your space perfect because you have an overwhelming fear of people coming over and judging you. Truly personal design has to come from a place of genuine interest in making your space beautiful for you and your family. Yes, it's fun to make it a game in which you attempt to one-up your neighbors, but the goal of all of this should be to have fun. And to be as perfect and happy as Gwyneth Paltrow in her glamorous home with its clean-ass floors.

OK, now that we've established that I don't think people should be allowed to keep anything on their kitchen counters and I am constantly afraid of being judged by my awful friends, let's get to the nitty-gritty of how to create a home that is intimidatingly formal AND also inviting.

MIXING AND MATCHING HIGH AND LOW

This is something that designers on dumb TV shows love blabbing about. But there is some real value in it. Adding a few formal accents (such as stripes on custom drapery) to some less formal elements (a farm-style coffee table) gives the room some seriousness while making sure it's not so serious that you feel like you need to be wearing a ball gown in order to enter. Although, if you're ever wondering whether to wear a ball gown or not, err on the side of wearing one. No one will ever get mad that you showed up to dinner at their house in a ball gown!

FANCY RICH PEOPLE HAVE UPHOLSTERED BEDS

An upholstered bed is the most luxe and comfortable type of bed available. I had a client recently who said he didn't like upholstered beds and I was so shocked my head basically fell off. If you are a human being with eyeballs and an epidermis, you should like upholstered beds. Like drapery and rugs, they add texture and softness to a bedroom. And the more softness a bedroom has, the more comfortable and inviting it will seem. So do you want a cold, hard bedroom? Or a soft cozy one? I'll let you decide.

UNEXPECTED ACCENTS KEEP THE EYES FRESH

The trick to making your space look preppy and formal isn't just to fill it with boring-ass preppy furniture. You have to have a few elements (such as the crocodile stool in the master bedroom above) to contrast with all the preppy, traditional furnishings elsewhere. Think of it as a palate cleanser. You know, the type you have at all the

fancy, formal dinners you go to since you are a glamorous, graceful, disgustingly rich reader of this book.

WAINSCOTING ALWAYS

Wainscoting, like in this beautiful staircase, is essential for any Cape Cod-style home. Or for any homeowner seeking a preppy, formal look. For those unfamiliar with the term, wainscoting is when the lower portion of a room has wood paneling. The structure of wainscoting gives the room an architectural strength that subtly tells your guests you are rich.

WHEN A ROOM WANTS TO BE DARK AND ROMANTIC

Sometimes you go into a space and you just know it should be a darker, more romantic space. Generally speaking, spaces that get less natural light tend to be good contenders. They are great for wood-paneled walls and saturated paint colors. In this home, the sitting room (previous spread) was just that type of room. It has great

windows, but because they're surrounded outside by trees there's never a lot of light in there. So we went with a saturated green wall color. Painting darker rooms a saturated color makes them feel intentionally romantic and moody, rather than dingy and gross like they'd look if they were just painted white.

A LITTLE STRIPE CAN GO A LONG WAY

Stripes are a great way to add some formality to a space. Incorporating them into accessories or foundational elements like drapery gives a little hint of elegance. Stripes should be the first step if you're looking to prep up your space. Added bonus: stripes are often used on prison uniforms, so using them in your home is a constant reminder that we are all prisoners in our own lives!

DIGNIFIED PEOPLE PRETEND THEY DON'T WATCH TV

I grew up without television, which is maybe where my aversion to having TVs in living rooms comes from. I try to keep television out of the living room if possible. If you can tuck it away in a den or a family room, away from your formal sitting area, it encourages a life where you don't necessarily just sit around watching TV as a default because it's in your face all the time. However, this isn't an option for everyone. My new place in L.A., for example, doesn't have an extra room for me to just plop a TV into, so I put the TV in the living room. Ideally, it's a good idea to make sure your television is grounded by having a media console under it. Or, even better, a built-in surrounding it. If you can afford it, a gorgeous built-in like the one above is a great way to minimize the soul-sucking impact of your television and make it look nicely integrated into the room.

CLASSIC COLORS KEEP THE SPACE LOOKING CLASSIC!

SHOCKER. Using traditionally preppy colors like navy blue and hunter green helps your space maintain that preppy vibe, while contrasting it with white trim gives the space some crisp formality.

A ROUND ACCENT TABLE CAN HELP FILL AN AWKWARD SPACE

Like me in my teenage years, some spaces in a home might be awkward, empty, and hard to engage. This type of space is the perfect candidate for a round table! Round tables make great accents in an entry area and provide a place to put your fresh cut flowers (WHICH YOU ALWAYS HAVE ANYWAY, RIGHT?). The round table helps soften the space by adding some curves to the otherwise rectangular room (previous spread).

WASPS CAN'T BEAR TO COOK ALONE

One thing I've learned from being part-WASP and from watching Nancy Meyers movies is that white people cannot bear to cook by themselves. So if you design a kitchen for a white person, make sure it's open to the rest of their home. This way, they can broadcast their white people problems (which are bound to be plentiful) to anyone who is within listening distance. Kitchens have become the epicenter of the home, so it's important your kitchen is large enough to fit the whole entire family.

WHEN YOU REALIZE YOU'RE LOSING YOUR MIND SO YOU MOVE TO SUBURBIA

WHAT IS SUBURBIA?

If you talk to me for more than six seconds, something you'll learn about me is that I was raised inside a national park—Yosemite National Park. Which is in California, NOT Wyoming. My parents both worked in the park (my dad was the dentist at the small clinic up there and my mom ran the little grammar school I attended, The Yosemite School). It was a magical childhood. My friends and I ran around like wild animals, playing with sticks and rocks as if they were actual toys. When I got older, we started venturing into the city every month or so.

Because I grew up in the woods and only went to cities, I never really understood suburbs. Which is why I found them so perplexing for most of my life. Until I saw the enormous Spanish home that is the subject of this section. The suburbs seem like a dystopian Pleasantville hellhole to all of us who have never lived in one. To me, it always seemed like to live in a suburb you had to be perfect at all times and that if you ever did anything wrong, a net would fall from the sky, capture you, and deposit you into a woodchipper. This is, of course, true, but there is also so much more to suburban life.

You might be shocked to learn that life in a suburb is actually pretty sweet. You get yourself some trees, some quiet, and there are a lot less people screaming directly into your face when you walk outside. The other important element of suburban living: SCALE, HONEY! You get so much bang for your buck when you aren't in the middle of a big-ass city. And let me tell you as someone who's lived in many a cramped New York and Los Angeles apartments, you reach a point in your life

where you're all "ENOUGH IS ENOUGH I'M TIRED OF MY SHOWER BEING IN THE KITCHEN!"

This gorgeous Spanish Revival home was my first major job after leaving Emily Henderson Design, and when I pulled up to the consult I was immediately terrified. Like many suburban homes owned by fancy rich people, this house is enormous. But I tackled my fears, designed this house, and it ended up being one of my favorite projects of all time. EVEN THOUGH WHEN I DID IT I LITERALLY THOUGHT I HAD NO CLUE WHAT I WAS DOING. So if you leave this book having learned nothing because all I did the whole time was make fun of everything and complain, I want you to think about this: DON'T BE SCARED TO TRY YOUR HAND AT DESIGN. YOU ARE ALREADY BETTER AT IT THAN YOU KNOW. ANY MISTAKE YOU MAKE CAN BE FIXED. YOU ARE A GODDAMN DESIGN GENIUS AND YOU CAN DO IT.

IS THE CITY MAKING ME INTO A CRAZY BAG LADY?

Years ago, I was standing on a subway platform in Philadelphia where I was living at the time, when I felt something on my foot. It was then that I realized the man next to me was peeing on me. On another winter day when I was living in New York, I was walking from my job in midtown Manhattan to my home in Chelsea when I stepped into one of those secret snow holes (you know what I'm talking about, like when you step off a curb into something that looks like snow but is really a huge puddle filled with snow/ice/sludge). At the same time, a huge bus drove by, splashing brown snow slush over my entire body and

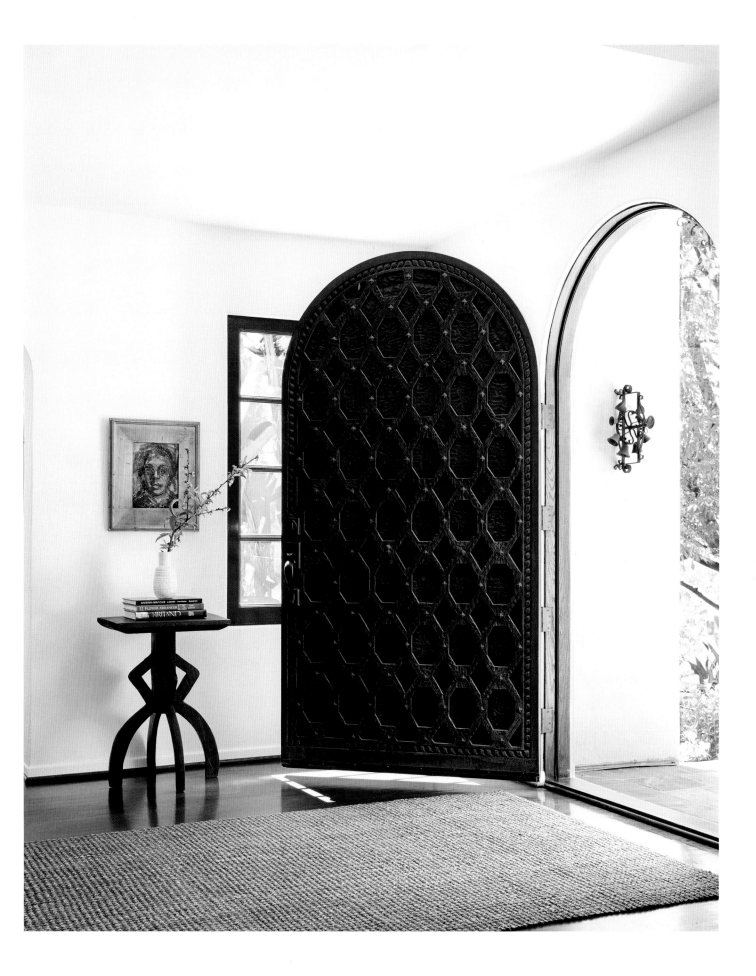

causing a gust of wind to blow a USED doggy waste bag directly into my face. In Los Angeles, where I currently live, there is a deranged man who lives near me and screams loudly directly into my face every time I walk out the door.

I'm not writing all this to complain (though let's be real, is there anything more fun that complaining?). I'm writing it to explain why people move to suburbs. Sometimes you just get sick of having your life be nothing but pain, misery, and gross-out stories. I get it. I feel like I might be trapped in cities forever, but I honestly get why people move to suburbs.

WHEN YOU WERE A LITTLE GIRL, DREAMING OF THE BIG CITY, YOU NEVER THOUGHT IT WOULD BE LIKE THIS

My childhood bedroom window looked out onto Yosemite Falls, the tallest waterfall in North America at 2,425 feet tall. I used to lay on my bed reading *The Andy Warhol Diaries*, dreaming of moving to New York City. And then one day I did, and it was awesome. But also gross. I think when you're twenty you're like, "Oh cool, that's gross," but then when you're thirty and you've been in the city a while you're like, "Why can't everything just be clean, like, all the time?" This is when it's time to move to the suburbs into a glamorous, giant Spanish Revival home outfitted with a mixture of vintage and new furniture!

LET'S FACE IT, EVERYTHING IS TERRIBLE

So yeah, it's time we all stop lying to ourselves, move out of the city, and get the giant-ass homes we all deserve. Instead, we think we're too cool. We think we need to be close to "culture" or whatever. But seriously, how many performances of the L.A. Phil did you go to this year? Have you ever even been to Lincoln Center? You're probably more likely to attend these performances if you had the time and serenity to plan going to them. THE TIME AND SERENITY YOU CAN ONLY GET FROM MOVING TO THE SUBURBS.

Look into my eyes. You've done your time. You're not getting any younger. If you stay in the city any longer you're going to turn into that crazy man who spit-screams into my face every day. IS THAT HOW YOU WANT FUTURE GENERATIONS TO REMEMBER YOU?

THE TIME HAS COME FOR *YOU* TIME

In designing a home with all the comforts suburbia has to offer, you should first think about how you will interact with the space and then think about all the amazing glamour parties you'll host there. Is the living room big enough to host a Christmas party for five hundred guests? Are there enough guest rooms for all your idiot friends who still live in the city? Is there adequate parking for all your guests out front? If not, is there a roundabout where the valet can be stationed? These may seem like trivial questions, but why move to the suburbs if EVERY SINGLE THING IS NOT EXACTLY PERFECT ALL THE TIME?

CREATING A COMFORTABLE FAMILY HOME SO YOUR KIDS DON'T TURN OUT TO BE DRUG ADDICTS AND STREETWALKERS

Choose the right style: many styles are compatible with creating a comfortable space for your family to live in so that your children will dominate in school, grow up to be insanely successful, move to the big city, and then ultimately move back to the same suburb you live in to be your very best friend. My favorite home styles are Spanish Revival, Craftsman, and Cape Cod. Therefore, these should be your favorite styles as well. I didn't invite you into this book so you could spend the whole time second-guessing me.

I've said it before and I'll say it again: creating a comfortable space for the ones you love is a way of showing your love and care for them. So your suburban home should be a reflection of your personality and the personality of everyone in your family. Allow space

for kids to play, make a space where dad can escape to contemplate his mortality. Create a space for mom to take her pills! When designing a home, think about how you're going to use it and work backward from there.

SOMEDAY YOUR CHILDREN WILL RESENT YOU FOR THIS

There comes a time in every child's life when she learns a very important lesson: how to resent mommy and daddy. This happens approximately at age fourteen, when your child will demand to start smoking cigarettes and wearing tube tops to school on a daily basis. You'll be like, "No, that's inappropriate for school and megatacky!" And she'll be like, "MOM, CHRISTINA WORE THE SAME THING ON TUESDAY AND NOW SHE'S CLASS PRESIDENT." And then you'll have to let her wear that ugly-ass outfit.

Kids who grow up in suburbia have more pent-up rage than your mountain or city kids. Because their whole lives have been about achieving a perfection that is only partially achievable, they grow up with an unparalleled psychosis about themselves and the world. For this reason, you need to make sure their suburban bedrooms are more inviting and comfortable than they'd need to be if you lived in a city or in the countryside. This is your duty. After all, you're the one that did this. You're the one that made them move to this goddamn forsaken place even though they totally would have loved to live on the Upper West Side and do drugs like the kids in *Gossip Girl*.

IF EVERYTHING ISN'T PERFECT, YOU'RE A FAILURE

If you are the owner of a gorgeous suburban home, one thing to remember is that if everything isn't perfect, you're a huge fuckup. I don't mean to worry you, but you absolutely must be perfect in all ways. This means that even the insides of your food pantry and serving ware storage rooms need to be perfectly styled. (What? You don't have an entire room dedicated to storing your serving ware? FIRED.) Moving to the suburbs is your chance to make everything in your life aesthetically perfect. DON'T FUCK IT UP!

SUBURBAN CASE STUDY: CREATING THE PERFECT SPANISH-STYLE HOUSE

As I said above, Spanish Revival is one of my favorite styles for gorgeous, suburban homes where you can escape from the city. You too can try this look and make yourself feel slightly more sane. The following are some ways to transform your house from STUPID to SPANISH.

ARCHES

One of the more distinctive features of Spanish Revival architecture is arched doorways and windows. This home began its life as a 1920s Spanish-style cottage, but underwent a massive renovation and addition. In order to keep the vibe truly Spanish, the homeowners made sure to include arches wherever possible. Now the beautiful entry door, many of the interior doors, and even some of the windows are arched. These arches tell your guests, I KNOW WHAT I'M DOING, STEP ASIDE!

WROUGHT IRON

Another distinctly Spanish Revival design element is wrought iron. In this home, we combined contemporary iron-finished light fixtures with more traditional Spanish Revival pieces. The rule we followed was that most typical room fixtures and those in pass-through areas were fitted with traditional lighting whereas larger, more communal areas with higher ceilings got contemporary fixtures that were in keeping with the traditional wrought-iron versions.

YOU DON'T LIVE IN A TIME CAPSULE

When working in a design style as specific as Spanish Revival, one's natural inclination is to make the whole place look like an old-timey museum. But adding in contemporary accents, as well as pieces from a variety of different origins, keeps your space from looking like the Spain section of Epcot. Just kidding there's no Spain section at Epcot, THAT

WAS A TEST AND YOU FAILED. Which should make you all the more dedicated to making your space look like it exists in 2018 (or whenever you're reading this) and not in medieval Spain.

TRICK 'EM WITH TRELLIS!

Trellis-patterned rugs are a great way to bring in some Spanish Revival style without being too obvious (opposite, far right). Trellis patterns mimic the aesthetic of Spanish tile, which gives your space an old-world, European vibe while keeping it youthful and fresh, LIKE YOU!

RICH, AGED LEATHER IS ALWAYS A GOOD ADDITION TO A HISTORIC HOME

My clients had this leather sofa long before I arrived, and while none of us were obsessed with its style, it's undeniable that, like my face, the leather has creased and

aged nicely over the years. Working it into their family room brings in some warmth and speaks to the historic tone of their home's style.

KNOW WHERE, WHEN, AND HOW TO BRING IN COLOR

Spanish Revival homes tend to look best painted all white. Adding in pops of color is a necessity if you don't want to die of boredom. This serving ware pantry (above) houses the family's collection of colorful glass dishes. (And yes, we all need a closet just for serving ware and it should be displayed beautifully at all times.)

HAND-DYED TEXTILES A DEF MUST

Homes with a historic style benefit from having handmade decor such as these throws and pillows (above). Why? Because historically (like in the olden days) people had to make things themselves or buy them from other people who made them by hand. This was before robots overtook humanity and stole all our jobs, forcing us to become Internet memes in order to survive. Handmade, hand-dyed textiles give a subtle hint at history and provide a warmth, individuality, and presence machine-made products lack.

WHEN YOU DESIGN YOUR DREAM HOME WITH YOUR BOYFRIEND THEN HE DUMPS YOU

WHAT IS LOVE?

I have only been to one therapist and he totally sucked and made me feel like an insane person so I stopped going to him. But speaking as my own therapist, I'd venture to guess that I have an insatiable desire for love and affection that's likely the result of being raised by new money forest people who somehow, strangely, were as aloof as old money Upper East Siders. My parents are the best people on earth, but they're super old-school and blue blood in a way. I was relatively independent as a kid. Not because I really wanted to be, but because it was what was expected/available. I'd be all, "PAY ATTENTION TO ME!" and they'd be like, "GO PLAY IN THE FOREST I'M READING." For this reason, I've spent my whole adult life seeking out the type of intimacy that my childhood lacked. I know this because I am my own therapist and I'm really good at what I do.

My expectation for my life was that I would meet the man of my dreams in college, we'd fall in love, have a fancy wedding, and be happy forever. I even planned my wedding. It's as follows.

THIS IS HOW YOU MAKE ME FEEL:

me→   you↑

MY WEDDING

BY ORLANDO SORIA

THE SETTING: Upstate New York, Autumn
DRESS CODE: Hedi Slimane Pour Homme (even on ladies)
SEATING FOR GUESTS: Hay bales

The wedding would go down like this: we'd be in the middle of the woods somewhere in upstate New York (I love this area because I went to college there and it's gorgeous). I'd be dressed in a tasteful drum major outfit leading a marching band/procession of all my besties. I'd march through the woods, the vibrant red leaves of sugar maple trees gently falling from above. Finally, I'd encounter a clearing where I'd find a group of people sitting on hay bales around a giant cake. I'd approach the cake, drumming along as the band played "Creep" by Radiohead. Finally, I'd reach the cake and just as I stopped my fiancé would pop out of the cake wearing nothing but a bow tie and an American flag Speedo. Then we'd get married by Joan Didion, who would spend the whole time saying poignant things about how the history of California's development relates to our love for each other.

HOW AWESOME DOES THAT WEDDING SOUND? It's stupid that I haven't gotten to do it yet. Like someone needs to marry me just so we can do this! I'm only half kidding when I say that this has been my wedding fantasy since I was twenty. Like I'd be totally down to actually do that.

So yeah, most of my adult life has been spent waiting for an extra special day. A day in which I'd run into a man on the street, I'd be holding books, of course, and we'd bump into each other and they'd fall on the ground. Then we'd lean down to pick them up and when we looked up our eyes would meet and that's when we'd fall in love. Then, as if by miracle, a spaghetti noodle would appear between us and we'd both be slurping on it until we kissed. I walk around all the time carrying books and cooked spaghetti noodles hoping this shit will happen but it never does. And it sucks because I haven't read a book since 2007. You should win a goddamn medal if you're reading this, to be honest. Most of the people who bought this book have given up and are just looking at the pictures by this point. But you. You stuck with it. Because you're better than all those garbage people. You're better than me, in fact. The only reason I'm writing this book is so that when people ask me what I've read lately I can honestly say, "I don't read books, I write them."

WHEN YOU KNOW YOU'VE MET THE ONE

I have a tendency to date emotionless robots and project all of my Disney love story fever dreams onto them. I'm not sure why I do this. I think I like to date people with no emotions because that's how I was raised and I'm used to being the codependent needy one with way too many feelings. So the last time I fell in love I was like, NO THIS IS NOT HAPPENING. Since this chapter is about relationships, I'm going to give the amalgamation ex-boyfriend character a name. We'll call him Logan. This is also my coffee name, which I give because if I give my real name the barista is all "FERNANDO? ARMANDO? GARBANZO? YOLANDA?" I don't think I'm very good at saying my own name, because no one ever understands what the fuck I'm saying. Anyway, fake boyfriend's name is Logan.

I fell in love with Logan 1 at a party because he could name all the artists in the art collection of the fancy mansion

we were in (I know, that's a gross reason to be impressed with someone but I was in my twenties). I fell in love with Logan 2 because he made a cute linguistic mistake (he was French but spoke perfect English, like better than me). He used to confuse "chill" with "chilled" so he'd be like, "Yeah I went to a party it was really chilled." It was very cute. I know this sounds condescending but I don't mean it to be (this is a person who speaks like four languages to my one). Somehow it was more possible to see his humanity when he'd make little mistakes like that. Like for a minute his polished, aristocratic front was gone and I saw someone who was once a little boy, someone vulnerable. These linguistic slips were very rare, but I cherished them in the three years we were together (and I never corrected him for fear he'd stop making them) because those moments were when I felt closest to him, when I felt like I saw him most fully.

Sometimes tiny things make you fall in love with people and there's nothing you can do about it.

HOW DO YOU KNOW WHEN IT'S TIME TO MOVE IN?

Logan 1 and I moved in together almost immediately because he was homeless-adjacent (check out the next section on page 63; I actually lived in that apartment with him but lied for the sake of that chapter and pretended I lived there alone. DON'T BELIEVE ANYTHING YOU READ IN THIS BOOK, GUYZ). I dated Logan 2 for almost two years before we moved into the apartment featured in this chapter. We knew it was time to move in because we slept over at each other's place every night for more than a year. It just didn't make sense to have two apartments anymore. I think this is actually a pretty good rule of thumb. If you never sleep apart and have been doing so for six months or more, it may be time to think about moving in together.

MY PLACE OR YOURS?

When contemplating a move-in, it's often pretty easy to figure out whose place to move into. Usually one member of a couple has a way better place than the other. In my case, Logan 2 owned his place, so it was obvious that I'd move in with him. But the place was a 1984 Formica mess. So before

we moved in, while I still had my apartment, we renovated his condo and lived at my place. I recommend this to all clients. If you can avoid living in your home while it's being renovated, do so at all costs. Living in a construction zone is a surefire way to fast-track your inevitable breakup.

For marketing purposes, and to get lots of things sponsored to offset the cost of the remodel, I gave the condo the name Orcondo. Yes, kinda weird since I didn't technically own it, but that's how the Internet works and also I literally cannot resist any sort of pun related to my name (Orblogdo, OrMomdo, Storelando, and hopefully someday, OrDogdo). We worked for about five months getting that remodel done and Logan 2 let me do basically whatever I wanted, so it was a really fun project. Renovating a home is a stressful experience that results in incredible bonding. Everything about it is an investment in an imagined future together. There's nothing more idealistic. It's a collaborative process in which the end goal is a perfect space where you can enjoy life and each other. Looking back on this still upsets me. Just thinking about how excited I was (we were?) about everything. It's hard not to temper excitement about the future when you can so clearly remember being excited about things that ended up ultimately being so painful.

EVERYTHING GOES, ALONG WITH WHATEVER'S IN THE ATTIC

One of the best things about moving in with a boyfriend is making him throw away all of the stuff he most cherishes. JUST KIDDING I NEVER DID THAT. But Logan 2 and I both got rid of a lot of stuff when we moved in together. I actually think constantly moving is a good way to make sure you never turn into a massive hoarder. I got rid of half of my belongings when I moved into Orcondo, and spent the next few years buying stuff until I moved out and got rid of everything again. I'm constantly shopping so I'm constantly getting rid of stuff. Normally I try to make my family take it but if they don't want it I donate it. I find that if I try to sell stuff it ends up taking so much time that if I paid myself an hourly wage for all the hours I spent selling it I would be making zero profit. My time isn't worth a lot, but it's worth more than that!

Long before Marie Kondo wrote about getting rid of your crap, I was advocating for getting rid of all your stuff. When I graduated from high school, I gave away nearly everything I owned, including my childhood teddy bear, Tofy. (Yes, he was named after tofu. This is California and I named him that when I was four.) When deciding with a partner what to give away and what to keep, it's important to make your partner think that everything is his idea. A fun fact about human nature is that people only want to do stuff if they think it's their idea. So if you want your boyfriend to get rid of his ugly ass lamp that I'm sure looked awesome in 1920s Paris but looks fucking awful in modern-day Silver Lake, be like, "That's nice Babe, not sure where we should put it yet." Eventually it'll end up near the front door, then it'll work its way to storage, then you'll never have to look at it ever again. If you'd been like, "I hate that lamp get rid of it!" he would have been like, "It's my favorite! I'm putting it in the bedroom!" People are dicks like that. All people.

Moving in together is a delicate balancing act at every step of the journey, including deciding what to get rid of.

THOSE ARE MY SCULPTURES, NOT MINE AS IN "I BOUGHT THEM" MINE BUT AS IN "I MADE THEM" THEY'RE MY SCULPTURES

One way to make sure your boyfriend loves you forever is to hide things you've made throughout the home. For this reason, I tried to make sure my art was all over Orcondo. From little sculptures on the shelving, to photographs I took hanging in the bedroom. This way, every time Logan 2 wandered around the apartment he'd think of me. This way, my identity would imprint upon his brain and then he'd want to be with me forever. And hopefully one day enact my totally awesome wedding idea (he could wear a French flag Speedo if he wanted). Unfortunately, this genius plan totally didn't work.

DOING CONTEMPORARY WITH BAE THE RIGHT WAY

I've never really been a fan of the word "contemporary" as it makes me think of ugly sectionals with chrome arms and high-gloss, alligator-skin-textured coffee tables. But contemporary just means "like what is current right now or whatever" (I believe that is the actual definition from the dictionary). So don't get weirded out by the use of this word. Many people say "modern" when they mean "contemporary." This is because we think modern means "modern times" when really it refers to a period of furniture design that happened around the '50s. If you call something "modern" you might be making a huge faux-pas if what you really mean is "contemporary." ARE YOU CONFUSED YET? "Modern" doesn't really mean "modern," K?

Anyhoo, now that I've assaulted you with a terminology lesson you totally didn't come here for, let's chat about contemporary design. The following are some surefire ways to make sure your contemporary casa doesn't turn out totally ugly and gross.

OPT FOR WINDOW TREATMENTS THAT GO AWAY
Contemporary homes are a great place to opt for simple roller shades with rectangular valances that blend into the streamlined architecture of the space and match the wall color.

DON'T OVERCOMPLICATE THINGS
Most minimal contemporary spaces are free from the types of moldings and accents present in more traditional homes. Thus, it's important to keep trim around windows and doors to a minimum. And when you do opt for moldings, make sure their edges are rectangular, not curved or overembellished like many moldings and trims

for traditional homes. However, just because the default is no trim doesn't mean you can't have a little fun with nontraditional uses of it. I added contemporary crown molding to the ceilings in the bedrooms by using materials traditionally used as baseboards. The effect was modern and elegant. LIKE YOU!

OPEN SHELVING ADDS CHARACTER

Adding open shelving in areas such as a TV lounge gives you the chance to display your collection of garbage-tchotchkes. If you don't have any garbage-tchotchkes, run out to the garbage store (thrift shop) immediately and buy some! Adding areas to display your accessories gives you the chance to add some character to your minimal space so that you can prove to your friends you're not totally boring/a murderer with no feelings.

CLEAN LINES DOESN'T MEAN BORING

Just because you want to keep the aesthetic angled and clean doesn't mean everything has to be hard-edged and alienating. Using pieces that have some softness to them, such as an upholstered bed, gives the space a welcoming feel that is still in keeping with the clean language of the home's architecture.

GO BOLD WITH LIGHTING

Because a contemporary space is inherently minimal, focal points such as ceiling light fixtures become more important than they might be in a space with more intricate architectural detail. So opt for light fixtures that make a statement. A statement like, "Hey, I'm sexy. Look at me."

CONTEMPORARY DOESN'T MEAN COLOR-FREE

While most contemporary spaces look best painted bright white, certain rooms can get away with a little splash of color. The master bedroom in this contemporary condo benefited from a navy-blue color splash. A general rule about this is that color can be a good idea if there is a natural stop (i.e., a door that closes that has a trim around it that creates a natural place for the color to end). The common areas in a contemporary space should likely be white, but bedrooms and bathrooms make great candidates for some color.

WHEN HE ALL "BOY, BYE"

One day, Logan 2 was acting aloof so I asked him what was up. He told me words that no one wants to hear from someone they love: "This just isn't working out." When someone dumps you, you kind of want to know why, but also don't want to know. The case with us was that I'd gained some weight and Logan 2 no longer found me attractive. As someone who's struggled with weight and body image issues my whole life, this was exactly what I needed to hear to fuel my self-hatred. The next few months were a nightmare.

Orcondo, once a symbol of a relationship growing and going in an exciting direction, felt like a jail. Logan 2 moved into the guest bedroom. I spent countless nights alone in the bed I'd custom-designed for us, staring at the ceiling unable to sleep while Logan 2 was out dancing. A few weeks later, Logan 2 went on a trip to Mexico with a bunch of single hot gay guys. I stayed in the condo alone, its stark minimalism having gone from soothing to depressing. Through my heartbreak I couldn't see any of the color I'd so carefully worked into the space. Everything was gray.

Interior spaces play a crucial role in our understanding of our own lives. They are a part of the family that goes unnoticed but emotionally impacts our daily lives, adding to our joy and to our pain. Orcondo was a space I'd spent years writing about on social media. Now it felt like a trap I couldn't wait to escape, a holding pen where I was forced to watch, like that gross eye-peeled-open scene in *A Clockwork Orange*, as the guy I loved happily went about his life without me.

You can never truly know what is going on inside your partner's head, regardless of how much you care for them. This is why one of the top Google searches is "Is my husband gay?" No one really knows anyone. Like you can know someone pretty well, probably way better than I knew either of my cagey-ass boyfriends. But you can never get inside their brains and know what's going on. Which is a bummer, because I'd like to know exactly what is going on in everyone's heads all the time. Otherwise, how can you figure out where your relationship stands? These are the thoughts that keep me awake at night. Now that I am single and lonely forever.

Relationships are built on trust. And I will never trust anyone ever again. So I'm in a great place.

EVERYTHING SUCKS, I'M EMO NOW, I HATE THE WORLD

I learned a few things from my past relationships. Mainly that men, including myself, are fucking assholes and that I'll never trust again. But I'm not bitter! (Yes, I am. Very, very bitter and angry. But in a cute, relatable way, not in an alienating, scary way. COME BACK PLEASE LOVE ME!)

Aside from learning to be totally bitter and angry at the human condition, I learned that cohabitating with a partner is incredibly rewarding and wonderful. Sure, I am now just a shell of the human being I once was, I'm dead inside, and it will take me years to recover and to be honest I never really will be able to truly love again, but I would do it again for sure. Why? Because it was really nice to be in love with those Logans. I have forgiven Logan 1, we were crazy together and I don't see him having a happy life anyway, so I dodged a bullet there. I'm in the process of forgiving Logan 2. I am actually a very nice person and try to always treat people the way I'd like to be treated. But for some reason I love holding grudges. It's hard for me to be like, "You were my family and you took yourself away from me so now I have nothing. I FORGIVE YOU!" No thanks.

One of my favorite slogans is "NEVER FORGIVE." In this time of New Agey nonsense about how we have to all be Zen and accepting of everything, sometimes it's nice to be like, "No, Ima hold that grudge because it's fun." So, yeah, I HATE BOTH Y'ALL LOGANS. Not that I'm like obsessing over it or anything. I'm just writing it down in a book for total strangers to read because maybe someone reading this has been recently burned and wants to hear from someone else who is still pissed. If you just went through a shitty breakup and you're reading this, know that I am pissed off on your behalf. LET THIS BE A LESSON TO ALL OF US TO HOLD ONTO OUR RAGE AS LONG AS POSSIBLE AND USE IT AS A MOTIVE TO MAKE OUR HOUSES AS PIMP AS POSS.

I am a professional interior designer and this is a very serious book about design and nothing I wrote above was TMI or unprofessional in any way and this section is over OK bye.

WHEN YOU FINALLY GET YOUR OWN PLACE AFTER LIVING WITH ROOMMATES FOREVER

I AM LITERALLY A BASTARD

Something my mom likes to remind me of all the time is that I'm a bastard. She likes to say from time to time, casually working it into conversation as she's cooking dinner or offering me a glass of Sonoma County sauvignon blanc, "You know, technically you're a bastard." I'm the youngest of three, so this means all three of us are bastards. Apparently the priest who married my parents forgot to send in the paperwork validating their marriage and my mother didn't find out about it until I was two years old. So I am literally a bastard. I have no idea if it's OK to even use "bastard" in this way anymore (like who cares if your parents were married before you were born?), but as a member of the Bastard Community I feel like it's OK for me to talk about. Like you can't make bastard jokes but I totally can. Sorry.

Why am I talking about being a bastard? Literally no reason. Aside from that I'm a complete and utter bastard.

I LIVED IN DORMS UNTIL I WAS TWENTY-FOUR AND THREE QUARTERS YEARS OLD

In addition to my bastard status, there are many troublesome things about me. One of my favorites is that I lived in dorms until I was almost twenty-five years old. I know that seems physically impossible, but it's true. To save money in both college and grad school, I worked as an RA. If you don't know what an RA is, it's the nerd who lives in your dorm who tells you not to smoke pot and gives you condoms. Luckily, I went to a liberal school so they didn't really make us yell at people about pot. Many famous people were RAs, including Hillary Clinton, Katie Couric, and Kerry Washington. But for the most part being an RA means you're just a huge loser with no friends who spends your weekends studying, in a constant state of panic that you might not get into your top choice law school (I wanted to go to law school, can you imagine?). When a grad student is an RA it's called a GA (Graduate Adviser), which is a title meant to mask how lame it is that you're twenty-three and live in a dorm with a bunch of idiot eighteen year olds.

But that didn't stop me. I just stayed in those stupid-ass dorms and acted like Dad for years and years and years. I spent all of college in a dorm, then ended up back in a dorm in grad school. So when I moved to L.A. when I was twenty-four and three quarters years old and finally had the chance to live in my own apartment, it was pretty much the most exciting thing to happen in my whole goddamn life. My first apartment was a little studio in Hollywood. Like no bedroom or living room or dining room. Just one room. But I loved it. I had no money to spend on anything so a friend of mine made most of my furniture for me. The rest of it was from thrift stores or that Swedish big-box bargain store that shall not be named.

BEING POOR TEACHES YOU STUFF

My first apartment taught me a lot about design and resourcefulness. I may have had literally zero dollars, but because I was creative and willing to try things out, my place looked beautiful. Your first place on your own is a great opportunity to figure out what your style is, what is important to you (style? comfort? PLEASE DON'T SAY COMFORT!). Your first foray into designing your own space is your chance to tell the world THIS IS WHO I AM. So don't mess it up!

The apartment in this section is NOT my first apartment. It's another one I moved into a few years after that. After I'd moved back to New York. Then back to L.A. Then back to New York. Then back to L.A. I did that like sixty times.

I'm one of *those* people. You know the type. The kind that just can't make up their minds. Finally I found a cute little apartment at the base of the Hollywood Hills and was like THAT'S IT I'M NEVER LEAVING. But I was still megapoor when I had this place, so I had to be creative with design decisions. LET THIS BE A LESSON TO ALL OF US THAT SOMETIMES WHEN OUR RESOURCES ARE LIMITED, OUR CREATIVITY GOES INTO BEAST MODE AND WE ACTUALLY CREATE MORE BEAUTY THAN WE MIGHT HAVE IF WE HAD ALL THE MONEY IN THE WORLD. Don't let your lack of dollars make you believe you can't have a pretty house. With a bit of time, sweat, dumpster diving, and hard work, you can create a gorgeous home on a budget. I BELIEVE IN YOU.

A FEW THINGS TO REMEMBER WHEN YOU MOVE INTO YOUR OWN PLACE AND ARE COMPLETELY ALONE IN THE WORLD WITH LITERALLY NO ONE TO LOVE YOU:

1. **EXPERIMENTING IS KEY.** You need to play around in order to figure out the best solutions to your design conundrums. Also, since you live alone there isn't anyone around to judge your tacky taste. YOU ARE ALL ALONE IN THIS WORLD AND THERE IS LITERALLY NO ONE THERE TO NOTICE IF YOU DROWN IN THE BATHTUB. In fact, upon your death, there's a 94 percent chance that you'll be in your apartment for days before anyone discovers your disgusting decomposing body. Don't be alarmed, but your decision to live on your own is a decision to live a desolate life filled with pain, misery, and loneliness. Your solo life will be unbearable. But you can walk around in your underwear so that's cool. In this apartment, one thing I wasn't sure about was this crazy gold Japanese screen (previous spread). It's not for everyone, but I knew I loved it. I wasn't sure it made sense in my bedroom until I added the gold pillow and the rug with ocher accents. All of a sudden it was like a big warm party in there. Sometimes you just gotta play until you find which of your home furnishings want to be friends with one another.

2. **FOLLOW YOUR HEART, BUT CHOOSE WISELY.** This just means you might not be able to mix all the styles you like because they may not be friends with each other. Some people just put everything they like together in a space without thinking about if it actually works together or not. You might love blue rugs, a blue sofa, and a purple vase (gross), but that doesn't necessarily mean they'll look great together. Before adding an element to a room, look at it next to what already exists in the space and see if it looks like it fits in. If it doesn't fit in, KICK IT TO THE CURB.

3. **ORGANIZE YOUR SPACE FOR CONVERSATION.** Make sure your living room has a completed conversation circle. Don't have all the chairs/sofas facing the same direction. Place chairs across from the sofa or next to the sofa on a 90-degree angle. This makes it easier for you to look your guests directly in the face when you beg them not to leave BECAUSE IF THEY LEAVE YOU'LL BE LEFT ALONE WITH NOTHING BUT YOUR EXISTENTIAL DREAD.

4. **EMBRACE ECLECTICISM.** Eclectic accents, such as gallery walls, add to a sense that your home was curated over time. They also bring in character and personality from around the world. A gallery wall, for example, combines the art of multiple artists into one space. Combining all these different styles and personalities will make you feel far less alone than you actually are. Because let's face it. You're all alone and no one is coming to save you if you accidentally puree your arm while trying to find a caviar spoon in the sink disposal.

5. **ART CAN BE A GREAT WAY TO BRING COLOR INTO A RENTAL WITHOUT LOSING YOUR DEPOSIT.** Landlords want to keep as much of your deposit as they can so they can spend it on lavish vacations and brand-new Mercedes. Bold large-scale art is the easiest way to make your place look gorgeous without changing the wall color. I made a large painting for my dining room, which was previously well-organized but totally boring and awful. It made the space like a million times more fun.

6. **OPT FOR GLASS IN SMALLER SPACES.** It may sound like a magic trick, but it actually does work. Using a glass dining or coffee table in lieu of a solid one can keep a space from looking too cramped. The transparency allows the eye to travel around the space and light to shine through. I'm not a huge fan of glass (it's cold to the touch and makes loud, shocking noises when dishes are placed upon it), but it is a great solution for any small space.

7. **THRIFT UNTIL YOUR EYES BLEED.** I found these side tables (see page 64) at a vintage store and immediately fell in love with them. Actually, that's a lie. An ex-boyfriend found them. But he's dead now (to me) so I'm going to take credit for sourcing these. If you're in a new place on your own for the first time, being resourceful and continually scouring flea markets and thrift stores is the best way to furnish your home without going broke.

Something to keep in mind when designing a space to live alone in is that you've just made a decision to live alone like a hermit and you're probably going to be overwhelmed with loneliness and misery. WHY DID YOU DO THIS? Didn't you know that solitary living is a road that leads directly to depression, binge eating, and to becoming such a social pariah that the mere thought of leaving the house fills you with overwhelming dread?

YOUR FURNITURE CAN BE GARBAGE JUST LIKE YOU

One trick I learned quickly upon graduating and moving out into the real world is that stuff for your house is EXPENSIVE. A sofa for $3,000?!? WHO KNEW! So you have to be smart about where you spend the dollars you don't have. Here's my rule:

SPLURGE ON ONE DISTINCTIVE PIECE THAT PEOPLE WILL NOTICE AND THEN FINISH THE SPACE OUT WITH JUNK FROM THE BARGAIN BASEMENT OR STUFF YOU LITERALLY FOUND NEXT TO A TRASH CAN.

One time, when I was living in Chelsea in New York City, I found a totally awesome FANCY BRAND NAME bookshelf on the street. I was like "DAMN GINA THAT'S GOOD." So I put it in my bedroom and felt SO rich. My actual adult, lawyer roommate thought I was a Garbage Pail Kid for doing it but I didn't care. I WAS POOR AS FUCK. You have got to do whatever you can to make your life as beautiful as possible, even if it means scavenging stuff off the street. People with unlimited budgets spend a lot of money to make their homes look like they're filled with leftover garbage looted from a sunken pirate ship. The cool thing about being poor is that all that supertrendy garbage you find on the street is actually chic. So don't think of your limited budget as an impediment. Think of it as a shortcut to being on the cutting edge of vintage-inspired design. In this case, EVERYONE WINS (except rich people who pay too much for vintage garbage that likely came from the same trash cans I like to dive in).

LOOK AT WHAT ARTISTS DO AND THEN DO THAT, BECAUSE ARTISTS ARE BETTER THAN YOU AND YOU KNOW IT

If you know any artists and you've been to their homes you know that their house is probably cooler than yours. Artists are better not only at composition, a key ingredient to creating a beautiful interior, but also at resourcefulness, which as we discussed is the number-one way for a poor person to get their house looking FLY. As I've gotten older (by the time you read this I will be a seventy-eight-year-old woman, with a rotting skeleton face, sitting on a rocking chair in Rancho Cucamonga, drinking Country Time lemonade, yelling maniacally at children as they pass by my house)…oh my god, that parenthesis got so long, sorry. Anyway, something I've noticed as I've slowly turned into a hag-witch from a Disney movie is this (in italics so you truly take it seriously):

Being an artist is hard. You have to figure out not only how to feed yourself and pay your rent, but also provide yourself a space in which to make things to hopefully show and sell to strangers. As a result, artists are insanely adept at figuring out how to organize things so they have a home, a space to create, and the ability to feed themselves while doing so. I've known a lot of artists and most of them live in pretty cool spaces. The reason (for the most part) wasn't that they had a ton of cash. It was that they weren't afraid to experiment with composition in their own home, to make things themselves, or to repurpose things they found or bought inexpensively. I'm not saying this to make it sound like all artists are deranged bag ladies who get all their furniture in the dumpster (I know some very successful artists). But artists tend to have an adventurous outlook on design. In the studio, artists get used to trying things, having them fail, and having to start all over again. What we can learn from artists is to have that same kind of adventurous spirit. To try things out and let go of our fear of failure.

We'd all do better to be more like artists. We need to make stuff. We need to scour flea markets and thrift shops. We need to have no shame about taking things out of the trash and making them into kick-ass home decor. If you want a SICK house, you gotta put in the time. If you don't wanna put in the time, you better be ready to put in the DIME.

IT'S A SMALL-ASS WORLD AFTER ALL

My final tip for you as you embark on designing your first solo home is to embrace global style. Add in accents from all over the world, so you will feel the art and culture from people all over the world as a replacement for any real human interaction you may have experienced when you had roommates or cohabited with a loved one (or someone who pretended to love you for a hefty savings on rent).

My mom spent a great portion of her childhood in Japan, so she was always like, "WE'RE JAPANESE!" Just kidding, she never said that. That would be racist and, quite frankly, it's pretty racist you even thought I was serious just then. She may not have pretended to be Japanese, but she did have a huge appreciation for the art and culture of that country, so I grew up with a strong love for Japanese design, which I carry with me to this day. If you think about it, the Japanese are better than everyone else at clean, minimal design that is also warm and inviting. Think about the simplicity of tatami mats and sliding screen doors. Ugh, I wish I were at a temple in Kyoto right now instead of this stupid coffee shop in Sonoma County where I'm writing. WHY CAN'T EVERYTHING ON EARTH JUST BE A BUDDHIST TEMPLE IN JAPAN???

One question I get a lot because of the strange pronunciation of my name ("Oar-Lawn-Dough" rather than "Or-LAN-Dough") is "EXCUSE ME WHAT RACE ARE YOU?" I am an American, like in the truest sense of the word, meaning that in terms of my race, nationality, etc., I'm an ambiguous mix of tons of different ethnic roots (Scandinavian, Spanish, Italian, Indian, Jewish, Mexican, British, literally everything), so I've never identified with any specific group. I've actually never really identified as a white person either because I was raised to identify as a Latino. I obviously look like a white person, but I've grown up with a

sense that I am a lot of different things and that has made me interested in learning about cultures around the world and celebrating their creations. I'd imagine if you're reading this you're the same. It's likely your family comes from all over, your influences and DNA do, too.

What I'm saying here is that seeking out global design influences is a good thing. It can feel daunting in this age of cultural appropriation to even think about having anything "ethnic" in your house. But as long as you're doing so in an inquisitive, responsible way, trying your best to learn about these objects and the cultures that create them, I say go for it. The future of our society depends on cultures being able to interact and appreciate each other, including a culture's art and design histories. You just have to make sure you don't have, like, looted objects or fake reproductions. Don't be all, "THIS FABRIC'S FROM AFRICA," only to have your friend look at it and go, "This says printed in China on it." Be smart, buy from dealers that are certified fair trade, and try to learn about what these objects are.

THAT CONCLUDES MY LECTURE ON CULTURAL APPROPRIATION AND INTERIOR DESIGN ACCESSORIES. MOVING ON.

DESIGN TIPS-N-TRICKS

Do you want your home to have a personality as awful as yours? Do you love gallery walls but have no idea how to hang one? Are you worried that your children are demons? If so, you've come to the right place! This chapter is about how interior design can help you solve all your terrible personal problems. I'll share with you my countless tips for creating stunning interiors in which you can live your best life. I may be a disgruntled mess, but you don't have to be!

PICKING A WALL COLOR THAT WON'T MAKE YOU BARF

YOU'RE RACIST

Before we can discuss wall color, we need to discuss your fear of The Other. Is your fear of color symptomatic of your fear of The Other? Is your need to keep all your walls white representative of your white supremacist views? People around town are saying your white walls mean you're totally racist. And not in like a mild, subconscious way. Like in a way where you should probably go to jail or something. As an anti-racist, I'm gonna need you to paint your walls a saturated color. Otherwise I'm gonna stand outside your house with a sign that says, "RACISM LIVES HERE."

OK FINE YOU'RE NOT RACIST

OK, maybe loving white walls doesn't necessarily mean you spend your spare time in a pointy hat and ghost costume. But it does mean maybe it's time to branch out. Adding color to your home makes life way more interesting. Scientists agree, people who have pigmented walls are ten times more likely to get a promotion at work and have sex lives that are 57 percent more satisfying than people with white walls. But how do we approach painting the walls a fun color? Keep reading and I'll tell you all you need to know!

WHEN IT'S ALL RIGHT TO BE WHITE

Now that I've railed against racism and white walls, I'm going to let you in on a little secret. Sometimes it's OK for your walls to be white! Below are some scenarios in which white is superior (if that sounded racist to you it is because YOU'RE racist, not because I said something that sounded racist, you should go look in the mirror and think about how terrible you are).

MODERN SPACES WITH LOTS OF NATURAL LIGHT

Contemporary homes that get a lot of natural light are great candidates for white paint colors. Generally, brighter rooms look better in lighter hues. If you have a room that naturally gets a lot of light, white or a lighter hue will probably look best in there.

SPACES WITH NO NATURAL "STOP"

In homes that don't have a lot of decorative moldings around doors, windows, and elsewhere, sometimes it can be difficult to create an elegant division between rooms painted in different colors. For this reason, it's often a good idea to paint these connected spaces white (or another neutral). There are exceptions to this rule, but moms generally agree it's best to keep these types of spaces white.

METHODS FOR ENSURING YOU DON'T MESS UP ROYALLY
Try Before You Buy

This is the number-one tip I give to everyone. You need to see the paint color IN THE SPACE before you commit to painting a whole room that color. The reason for this is that many factors go into how a color will read in a space: lighting (is it warm or cool?), wall texture, flooring and other colors in the room, and time of day. I had a (gorgeous VIP celebrity) client recently whom I chose a beautiful gray paint color for. When we painted the walls, it looked baby blue. The reason? To save money, we left the ceiling and trim painted the warm milky white color it was when she moved in. The white color that was there had so much yellow in it that it made the gray look blue by contrast (yellow and blue are opposites on the color wheel so sometimes putting yellow next to something neutral will make it look blue).

JUST BECAUSE THE WALLS ARE WHITE DOESN'T MEAN YOUR HOUSE HAS TO BE TOTALLY COLORLESS. TRY ADDING A FUN POP TO THE DOOR OR TRIM!

THIS ROOM IS PAINTED ONE OF MY
GO-TO PAINT COLORS, SLEIGH BELLS
BY BENJAMIN MOORE

In fact, it's kind of important to understand the color wheel in order to anticipate how colors will interact:

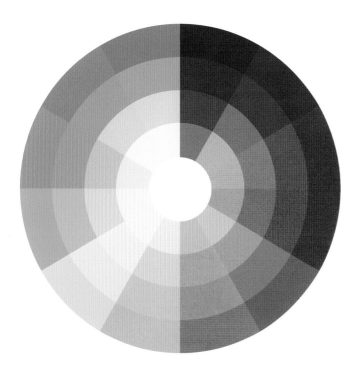

Keep this color wheel in mind when thinking about colors. For example, if you paint your walls a beige that has a lot of red in it, be careful to also use a warm enough paint color for the trim or it may end up looking green. COLOR IS CONFUSING. I literally spent six years in art school mixing paints in order to understand it better, so it's totally fine if none of this makes sense to you. If you feel perplexed, it's probably best to give up and hire a designer. If you can't hire a designer, just use these classic gray colors (I use them all the time and they NEVER fail):

FOR BRIGHT ROOMS: Benjamin Moore Horizon walls with Benjamin Moore Super White trim/ceilings

FOR MEDIUM-LIT ROOMS: Benjamin Moore Sleigh Bells walls with Benjamin Moore Super White trim/ceilings

FOR DARKER ROOMS: Benjamin Moore Half Moon Crest walls with Benjamin Moore Super White trim/ceilings

I have never had these colors backfire, because they are pretty classic/true grays, not too warm, not too cool. But please adhere to my rule before you paint anything, TRY BEFORE YOU BUY.

How to Test Your Paint Color

There are a few methods I like to use to test out different colors before I put them on the wall. The first is the most basic. Using a paintbrush and your human arms, paint your color(s) onto the wall in a 12-inch square. You can procure sample pots of paint from most hardware stores so you don't have to commit to buying a whole gallon. The next method is to paint your colors onto a self-adhesive paint color test sheet that can be applied to the wall. You can get these at a hardware store as well. For both these methods, make sure to use at least three coats of paint so you can see the true color. I like to try 3–5 colors per room. If you're going for a specific color, try that color, a warmer version of the color, and a cooler version of that color.

Desaturate, Desaturate, Desaturate

Usually when people choose paint colors, they go for a color they love. Normally, that color is bright and vibrant and exciting. I'm telling you right now, YOU DON'T WANT THAT COLOR IN YOUR HOUSE. It seems like a good idea, but it's going to look like Mickey's Toontown and you are going to lose your mind in a matter of seconds. The key to creating a home that looks sophisticated enough for an actual grown-up to live in is to select your color, then look for a SUPER DESATURATED version of it. Desaturated just means a lot subtler, more gray and neutral tones, less vibrant. I know this sounds boring but putting full-on bright-ass colors in your house is a surefire way to make you projectile vomit every time you look at your wall.

Get to Know Your Walls

In choosing the right finish for the right space, you're going to need to have an understanding of the wall texture you're working with. Generally, walls that are more fucked up should be painted a flat finish. And by "fucked up" I mean that they are highly uneven, have a lot of patched holes, and are generally not smooth (this is basically every wall in every apartment I've ever lived in). The higher the gloss of

paint, the more apparent flaws in the wall's texture become. So while the high-gloss look is totally in right now, it only looks good on walls that are perfectly smooth.

Types of Finishes and Where They're Appropriate

FLAT: Bedrooms, dining rooms, living rooms, libraries, basically anywhere with a fucked-up wall.

MATTE: Same as above, but with slightly less fucked-up walls.

EGGSHELL: This is where you start getting fancy. Like your walls are nice enough that they can have a bit of sheen without looking like my busted acne teenage face.

SATIN: This paint finish works in kitchens and bathrooms, but isn't quite as easy to clean as the next two types of paint. Keep reading.

SEMIGLOSS: This is typically what is used for trim, bathrooms, and kitchens. It works well for kitchens because you can splash spaghetti sauce all over everything and it'll just wipe off. So either stop living like an animal or paint your kitchen semigloss.

HIGH GLOSS: This is either for superfancy rooms where you want the walls to look like patent leather, or for disgusting dirty rooms where you plan on living like a pig (like the kitchen or bathroom). High-gloss brings in a different texture and a sense of sophistication. If you can pull it off (which is unlikely, to be honest), it can be a fun accent for a foyer or nursery for a particularly superficial and/or fancy baby.

TRY NEW THINGS

Painting is one of my favorite inexpensive ways to update a space. I love it because it's one of the more accessible ways of beautifying your home. For about $30–$50, a gallon of paint will completely transform a room. There are few other interior design tricks that give you so much bang for your buck. So it's definitely not something to freak out about or overthink. If you hate the color you paint a room you can always change it. And, if you can't afford to hire a painter, painting itself is good core exercise. So not only will it make your home look like a million bucks, it'll also transform your body from FLAB to FAB in only twenty minutes. I GUARANTEE IT! Or your money back! Just kidding PLEASE do not return this book. I'm relying on the income (so I never have to move in with my parents again).

OK bye. Go paint!

HANGING ART SUCKS LET'S DO IT TOGETHER

HANGING ART IS TOO HARD AND YOU CAN'T DO IT

My years of working as a professional, high-powered interior designer have taught me a lot of things. But the most important thing I've learned is that there are three things I hate doing:

1. Hanging drapery (I refuse to do it anymore)
2. Moving/touching a rug and/or a rug pad (I can't deal with the texture of rug pads)
3. Hanging art (ESPECIALLY GALLERY WALLS)

If you hire me to design your house, I will most definitely hire someone else to do those three things. I'm happy to help you move your sofa across the room (that's basically like a free CrossFit workout!), but I'll literally slap you across the face if you ask me to do any of the above. So everything we're gonna chat about right now is a hypothetical. I hate hanging art and so can you!

WHY GOD?!? WHY IS IT SIMULTANEOUSLY SO BORING AND ANNOYING?

Why do I hate hanging art, you ask? Well, I'll tell you. It's a combo of things I hate: math, fretting, worry, preplanning, and precision. I hate math so much that when I got to high school I was placed in Math for Idiots and everyone else in the class was missing their front teeth and chewed on straw the whole time while looking cross-eyed into space (I went to high school in a terrifying horse town where everyone married their sister, sat on the backs of their trucks all the

time, and knocked over cows for fun. I'm clearly still bitter about it). The only math I'm good at is geometry, which I'm kind of great at. But geometry only plays a small portion in art hanging. Mostly it's just adding and subtracting, which I'm too stupid to do. A sad fact about me is that I was only smart for exactly ten years, from 1996 to 2006, the years when I needed my brain for school. Like just smart enough to get into college and do amazing in it, then I graduated and smartphones came out and now I'm a total fucking idiot because I don't do anything except look at screens all day. LET THIS BE A LESSON TO ALL OF US TO PUT THE GODDAMN PHONE DOWN OR YOU'LL END UP LIKE ME, ONE STEP UP FROM HAMSTER INTELLIGENCE. VICTIM.

I think what freaks people out about art hanging is that it feels so permanent. Like picking out the right tube top before a hot night out on the town, hanging art can feel like a terrifying, permanent move that affects the rest of your life. But one needn't be scared. I am going to outline some ways for to you deal with your commitment fears.

WHAT'S THE RIGHT WAY TO HANG STUFF JUST KIDDING THERE ISN'T ONE

The most important thing to keep in mind while hanging art is that you're doing it wrong. AND THAT'S OK! Why? Because there is no RIGHT way to hang art! Historically, scientists and art historians have agreed that hanging your art so that its center is 58 inches high is correct. BUT WHAT IF YOU'RE TWO FEET TALL? That hanging height doesn't sound so great now does it? OR WHAT IF YOU'RE EIGHT FEET TALL? Then the art would be too low if it was hung at 58 inches. Are those scientists and art historians saying there's something wrong with being two feet tall or being eight feet tall? FUCK YOU SCIENTISTS AND ART HISTORIANS LET US LIVE OUR LIVES, CELEBRATE DIVERSITY, AND BE FREE.

What I mean to say here is that the correct way to hang art depends so much on what you are hanging, where you are hanging it, who you are hanging it for, and a variety of other factors. So I'm not about to come into your house to make huge general rules about how you should hang your art. I'm your friend, I'm not here to oppress and dominate you. That's what scientists and art historians are for.

WHEN IN DOUBT, HIRE SOMEONE

Before you get started hanging your art, think long and hard. Is this really how you want to spend your Saturday? Sweating and yelling at the ceiling? Why not inflict that pain upon someone else by finding a handyman or art installer to hang your art for you? That way, you can avoid physical labor, contribute to the economy by hiring someone for a task you could very well do yourself, while you sit back and drink a nice, cool glass of lemonade and/or straight-up vodka while thinking about how your feelings are more important than everyone else's.

I'm serious. Think about all the struggles you've faced in your life. All the setbacks you've had. How hard it's been to get where you are. How many people tried to step on you along the way, to hold you down. How many times did you fail before you prevailed? You are a wildly successful businesswoman, but you started from nothing. YOU REALLY WANNA GIVE THAT ALL UP AND HANG YOUR OWN ART? AFTER ALL YOU'VE BEEN THROUGH?!?

OK fine. Try it. But don't come crying to me when you fuck it up. It's inevitable that you're going to fuck it up. And when you do, I hope you'll remember that I told you it was going to happen. You were destined to be an art hanging failure from DAY ONE.

K fine. Do what you want. I thought we were friends or whatever. Guess I was wrong.

TOOLS YOU'LL NEED

1. Hammer
2. Screws
3. Art hangers (those brass things you nail into the wall that look like little baby hooks)
4. Spackle
5. A putty knife
6. Touch-up paint
7. A pencil
8. A measuring tape
9. Blue painter's tape
10. Sandpaper
11. A sense of adventure!

IF YOU INSIST, THIS IS HOW YOU HANG A STUPID-ASS PIECE OF ART

1. Decide on height. I often like to hang art at kissing height. Meaning if I'm standing right in front of it, its center is at mouth height, so I can French-kiss it when I feel like it. If you don't like your art enough to want to French-kiss it all the time you should buy new art. I make out with mine all the time. Remember, typical gallery/museum height is 58 inches. BUT DON'T LET THOSE ART TYRANTS TELL YOU WHAT TO DO. DON'T LET NO MAN TELL YOU WHAT TO DO. NOT TODAY NOT EVER!

2. Mark the wall at the midpoint of the top half of the piece you want to hang.

3. Measure the distance between the hanging wire/hardware and the top of the piece.

4. GODDAMN THIS IS BORING.

5. On the wall, measure down from your previous measurement (2), marking the distance between the hanging hardware and the top of the piece (3).

6. CAN WE DRINK NOW? WHAT KIND OF ROSÉ DO YOU HAVE?

7. Use a nail to install your art hanger so the hook is at the height of your lower mark (5).

8. SERIOUSLY DO YOU HAVE BOOZE? OR MEDICAL MARIJUANA OR SOMETHING? IS THERE, LIKE, AN UBER FOR DRUGS? I HATE THIS LIFE I JUST WANT TO FORGET EVERYTHING.

9. Using your human hands, hang your art on the art hanger you've just installed.

10. Stand back and enjoy your freshly hung art.

11. Get closer, caress the art.

12. Go in for the kiss, French-kissing the art tenderly and passionately.

13. LEAVE THE ROOM AND GO ON A DRUG/ALCOHOL BINGE FOR APPROXIMATELY THREE WEEKS.

DIRTY TRICKS RICH STYLISTS USE AND NO ONE ELSE KNOWS

Did you know that stylists make up 45 of the Top 50 Forbes Billionaires List? And that stylists are 8 percent more likely to own their own private islands and have more satisfying lives than you? It's true. While I'm not a true stylist, I've delved into the field enough to learn some of their rich people tricks. I'm gonna share those tips with you now and BLOW YOUR MIND.

1. For lighter art, try removable adhesive hooks. These don't work with all art, but for lighter art and stuff you don't plan on leaving up forever, they're a great way to hang art without a hammer. And let's face it, WHO REALLY WANTS TO TOUCH A HAMMER?

2. Art LOVES wiggling around on the wall and getting all wonky. They sell products for this, but they tend to be all gooey and gross. I just use a small rolled up piece of blue painter's tape to adhere the bottom of the frame to the wall. And there you go! No wiggling! It's a simple/fast way to get your art under control.

3. I guess I only have two stylist tricks. Sorry.

OK FINE, WE CAN TALK ABOUT GALLERY WALLS BUT I'M GONNA HATE IT

I have been hired by countless clients because they loved one thing from my portfolio: GALLERY WALLS. If you look at the *Dictionary of Things Orlando Hates to Do*, "Hanging Gallery Walls" is pretty high up there. I'm actually fine doing them for myself. But doing them for clients is another story. Why? Because there is one secret to creating the perfect gallery wall and if clients knew it they would FREAK THE FUCK OUT. What is that trick? I don't think you can handle it. It's a lot. You sure you wanna know? Like really sure? OK fine, here it is.

THE KEY TO CREATING A BEAUTIFUL, ORGANIC, NATURAL GALLERY WALL IS TO HAMMER AND NAIL THE FUCK OUT OF YOUR WALL UNTIL IT LOOKS LIKE SWISS CHEESE.

See? I told you you didn't want to know. I've tried method after method after method and really the best method to making a gallery wall look great is just making tons of holes in the wall. Like so many holes that the room is no longer structurally stable. Gallery walls are the reason that all my previous apartments have walls composed of roughly 97 percent lightweight spackle that would immediately implode in an earthquake, killing everyone.

The reason for all these holes? It's pretty much impossible to get gallery wall hanging right the first time. Given that there's so many variables: multiple pieces of art, different hanging hardware with different distances between the top of the art and the hardware, different tools required to install different types of art (screws, nails, picture hangers, etc.), it's literally impossible to get

ELEMENTS OF A PROPER GALLERY WALL

+ Equal rivers (spaces between art)
+ Mixture of scales (large and small equally distributed)
+ Mixture of frame styles/colors
+ Distribution of mediums

SIGNS YOUR GALLERY WALL IS WHACK

+ Unequal rivers
+ Crooked art
+ Scale not distributed (all the big pieces together, all the small pieces together)
+ Upside-down art
+ Art randomly hanging far away, feeling lonely

hanging right the first time. And given that a gallery wall consists of many pieces of art, you'll have to make about four hundred thousand holes in the wall before everything is hung at the perfect height/distance from each other. So, before you decide to hang a gallery wall, you should ask yourself, "Is this gallery wall worth my house falling over on top of me if it gets too windy?" For most of us design lovers the answers is an obvious yes (FUCK YOU PRACTICALITY!), but it is a decision you need to make. ARE YOU WILLING TO DIE FOR A GALLERY WALL? Again, for me the answer is an obvious yes, but that's a choice you'll have to make for yourself.

DON'T BE SCARED, WE'RE ALL GOING TO DIE ONE DAY

If you've learned one thing from this chapter, it's that if you are attempting to hang art you should be scared out of your mind. It's very unlikely you'll be able to do it well, if you can even do it at all. But just remember, make as many holes in your wall as you want. Mistakes don't matter. Mistakes are why God invented spackle (if only you could spackle over your twenties, AMIRIGHT?). Just remember, you're doing it wrong and that's all your fault. But someday all your hole-filled walls are going to come crashing down on you and none of this will matter. SO HAMMER AWAY!

SELECTING A RUG THAT'S NOT A HUGE BITCH

There are lots of really difficult decisions to make in life. Should you go to prom with Brad, who's cute but kind of stupid? Or should you go with Greg, who's totally nerdy but will one day blossom into a successful entrepreneur and get totally rich and buy you so much pottery? Should you invest your bonus in a mutual fund or should you invest in a new face and hope that a random person from the Internet sees it and decides to buy you online so you can move to his giant house in Texas? He'll be out taking oil meetings or whatever all day, you'll be home arranging flowers and playing the piano. It'll be great. You'll be so rich and all you'll have to think about is which Pilates class to go to and who to invite to your next dinner party. So yeah, in that case definitely opt for the plastic surgery/new face situation over the mutual fund. Mutual funds are dumb and boring.

Some decisions are much easier to make than others. Rugs, for example, are something you should not be afraid to bite the bullet on. Before we get into the nitty-gritty of selecting rugs, let's chat about rugs in general.

YOU NEED A GODDAMN RUG

If you're wondering whether you need a rug or not, YOU NEED A GODDAMN RUG. Almost always the correct answer to the question "does a rug belong here?" is "YES, STOP YOUR DITHERING, GET OFF YOUR LAZY ASS, AND GET TO THE STUPID RUG STORE TO BUY A RUG." I say this because I have a lot of people in my life who don't understand why they need rugs. They're all, "I just redid my floors, I want to see the pretty wood." And I'm like, "SHUT UP. NO ONE WANTS TO BE IN THIS ECHO-Y ASS ROOM WITH NO MOTHERFUCKING RUG." And then I slap them, they come to their senses, and we both look into the camera and go, "THANK GOD ORLANDO'S HERE!" [*tooth sparkle*].

MEN ARE ASSHOLES

It's especially an issue with dudes. I have no idea if any straight men are reading this book (if you are, you are probably a member of the coolest subset of men on earth, you get it and you're cool and all the other straight guys are lame and boring). Guys don't seem to get why you should have rugs. The reason is COMFORT AND JOY. Rugs do the following:

1. Create a defined space in which your furniture can live together in harmony.

2. Adds texture to the room. More texture equals more complexity equals a more balanced, eclectic space.

3. Absorb sound. Do you really wanna sit next to your boyfriend as he crunches on chips, the deafening grinding of his teeth vibrating your bones until it's all you can do to keep yourself from stabbing him over and over?

4. They make cozy on your toe-toes. Let's face it, it's much more comfortable to sink your toes into a nice, high-pile rug than into a hard, impenetrable concrete/wood/whatever floor.

5. Rugs are great sound buffers that help muffle the sound of your heavy elephant stomping feet. I tend to stomp my feet wherever I go. My ex used to be like WHY ARE YOU WALKING SO LOUDLY and then I'd try to tiptoe but Jesus tip-toeing is boring and makes you feel like a gay stereotype from the '20s, *"DID SOMEBODY SAY ASCOT!?! My wrist just went limp!"*

Have I convinced you that you need a rug yet? GOOD. Now that that's over, let's talk about how to choose the right rug for the right space.

SIZE MATTERS

Number one, we needa talk about scale. A lot of people are all, "IS THIS RUG BIG ENOUGH?" And I'm like, "No, you just put a welcome mat in the middle of your living room and asked it to be an area rug. IT NEEDS TO BE BIGGER." Too-small rugs are the number-one mistake people make, aside from marrying the wrong person or repeatedly seeking out partners who criticize them. Not that that's ever happened to me. BACK TO RUGS. Don't get one that's too small. It's going to piss off all your guests and make everyone think you're poor. Not that it's bad to be poor, but if you can, buy a rug that doesn't make everyone feel sorry for you. Rules are stupid, but here are a few rules I like to follow for rugs:

1. In a living room, the rugs should be big enough for the front legs of the sofa to sit fully on it. Bonus if the entire sofa fits on the rug. Double bonus if *all* the furniture fits on the rug. LITERALLY EVERYONE'S INVITED TO THE PARTY.

2. If a space is carpeted, make sure to select a rug that is a different texture/color than the carpet you are laying the rug over. For example, a flat woven kilim rug usually works over a medium-pile carpet. Don't do a medium-pile rug over a medium-pile carpet. Just like it's important to celebrate diversity in everyday life, the same is true for rugs—the more distinct the better!

3. When considering a rug's color, think about what its function in the room is. Is it there to be the pop of color? If so, go for a saturated hue. If you have a lot of other color going on in the room, maybe prevent it from looking like a 3-ring circus by choosing a more muted rug.

4. Hallways love rugs. A runner is a hallway's best friend.

5. Kitchens also love rugs. Vintage rugs make especially good kitchen rugs because no one will be able to tell when you spill grandma's spaghetti sauce all over it.

6. Get your rugs cleaned once every year or two. Most cities have drapery/rug cleaning shops. If your city doesn't, get on your hands and knees and scrub until your fingers bleed.

7. Choose the right shape for the right room. Most rooms are rectangles, so they want rectangular rugs. But sometimes a round rug makes more sense. My dining room is a good example of such a space. It's a small, square space, so using a round rug added a little bit of movement.

WRONG, WRONG, RIGHT

These three rugs show two bad options and one good one. The round rug is cute, but the wrong shape. Round rugs are generally best for pass-throughs and square rooms where a rectangular rug would look awkward. The small rectangular rug is too small for the space, will feel dwarfed by the

furniture, and will be almost completely covered by the coffee table. The final rug is the right size and proportion for the room because it covers a large portion of the space while leaving some breathing room around the edges. There's no hard, fast rule on how much space you should leave around a rug, but I like to make sure there's at least 12 inches on all sides. Additionally, it's important to make sure furniture pieces like dressers and media consoles are on the wood floor, not layered over the rug so make sure to take that into account when determining a rug size.

DON'T MAKE THE SAME MISTAKE I DID

You guys, confession time. We all make mistakes and I have totally made mega millions of them. Take this living room above, for example. The rug I originally sourced for it was way too small. For some reason I tried to squash the whole sofa onto the rug. Correct solutions here would have been to reorient the rug so that only the front legs of the sofa were on it or get a bigger rug. After this photo was taken, this rug was replaced with a larger rug the whole sofa could fit onto. And all was back to better! But I'll always live with the secret shame of smashing this sofa onto a rug and allowing it to be photographed. That kind of mistake follows a designer to his grave. DON'T LET YOURSELF BE VICTIMIZED BY THIS TERRIBLE MISTAKE LIKE I WAS.

DO YOU HAVE A RUG YET?

People think rugs are accents, but they're vital to making your space feel like a comfortable interior and not a cave infested with rats and inhabited by barbarians. So buying a rug is not something you can just put off forever. Every day you live in your house without a rug, your soul dies a little bit more. You may not notice, but not having a rug is taking years off your life and damaging you spiritually. So get it together and get yourself some rugs PRONTO!

BE INTENTIONAL. MAKE SURE YOUR FURNITURE INTERSECTS WITH YOUR RUG IN A WAY THAT LOOKS LIKE YOU DID IT ON PURPOSE. THIS MEANS EITHER OVERLAPPING THE FRONT OF YOUR FURNITURE ON TOP OF THE RUG OR MAKING SURE THERE IS SPACE IN FRONT OF YOUR FURNITURE FOR SOME BREATHING ROOM AROUND THE RUG.

INTERGENERATIONAL RELATIONSHIPS: MIXING AND MATCHING VINTAGE AND NEW

A space doesn't seem quite right when it's filled only with brand-new furnishings. For me a home doesn't feel done until there are some vintage items present. Why? I think it's because vintage furniture and accessories bring a history and age with them that is impossible to replicate, even with the best faux finishing on earth.

One of the homes in this book (the Spanish Revival home in Chapter 1) is half-original, half-new construction. The older part of the home was built in 1935 and the new addition was built in 2010. Even though the new portion of the home was built with exacting detail to match exactly the style of the original structure, using the same historic materials, the new portion of the home feels different than the older portion of the home. When you walk into the music room, which was part of the original 1935 build, you can feel a difference. It's difficult to explain, but there's just a different essence to the older portion of the home. This is why Americans love going to Europe so much, seeing all these old structures that have so much presence and history to them.

Objects and furniture have the same type of inexplicable powers of attraction. Vintage pieces, much like vintage homes, give off a historic presence that gives your home a warmth and complexity that new objects cannot. I like to balance vintage pieces with newer items to make sure the space feels full of character but also fresh. But many people find vintage shopping to be totally daunting and overwhelming. Below are my tips for finding the best vintage pieces.

LOOK LOW, LOOK HIGH (BUT MOSTLY LOW)

There are a lot of gorgeous showrooms that sell only the best vintage treasures. If I could afford to shop only in those places, I would. But for someone getting started in the vintage game, I'd stick to thrift shops and flea markets. There's a Goodwill down the street from me that I go in almost every time I pass it. Eight out of ten times I find nothing, but occasionally I find something amazing. It's a constant search. I still love going into high-end vintage and antique dealers, both for inspiration and on the off chance I can afford something in there. The more you spend on something, the more of a commitment it is. So dipping your feet in the thrift store/flea market pool is an unintimidating way to get started collecting vintage.

FOLLOW YOUR INSTINCTS

When shopping, sometimes you don't know if you love something until hours later. But if it's a flea market that may mean it's too late. I tend to think that if you find yourself attracted to something, you should follow your instincts. I've had so many traumatic experiences at flea markets where I second-guessed myself only to realize later I passed up something awesome I totally should have snatched up. Usually your first impression of something is correct.

DETERMINE YOUR QUIRK QUOTIENT

The tough part about vintage is there's a thin line between things that are awesome and things that are just tacky and gross. The easiest way to figure out if a vintage object is cool or disgusting is to imagine it styled on a bookcase with a stylish combination of new and old items. If it seems like something that will look great next to a bunch of other pieces, it's probably awesome. If it looks like it's gonna stick out like a sore thumb, it's probably not a good buy. Take, for example, this little wooden duck bowl (above). It's definitely weird, but when placed on a stack of books, on an elegant dresser, its quirkiness creates the perfect contrast to the sophisticated things surrounding it.

LOOK FOR HANDMADE

While art from galleries and high-end boutiques can be very expensive, sourcing vintage art from thrift stores is a great way to grow your collection. While you might not be buying art by megafamous artists, this is a great way to find beautiful, handmade items that add personality to your home.

IF IT'S AWESOME, IT'S WORTH RESTORING

When I found this wooden bird candelabra (previous spread) at a thrift store, his beak had broken off and he was sad and all alone. So I paid the $4.99 he cost, took him home, and made a new nose for him (by filing a wooden dowel down

using a pencil sharpener). If something is amazing and unique, it's worth a little effort to restore it.

SEARCH FOR ITEMS THAT WORK WELL TOGETHER

My ex-boyfriend and I found these two different busts (above) at a flea market and I knew immediately that they were meant to be together. I was so committed to their pairing that I gave them to him when I moved out because I couldn't bear to see them separated. When planning what pieces you want to pair, think about mixing materials and making sure they are different heights (when grouping things it's usually a good idea to make sure objects are different heights).

GOING VINTAGE CAN BE A GREAT WAY TO SAVE ON FOUNDATIONAL ITEMS

Pieces like dressers, side tables, coffee tables, and other non-upholstered items can be found at flea markets and

thrift stores at great prices. I exclude upholstered items here because they often need to be reupholstered, which can add significantly to their cost. Most of the dressers I've ever bought have been vintage. If they're made out of quality wood and have been well taken care of, they'll last forever.

FRAMING VINTAGE ART MAKES IT LOOK WAY IMPORTANT

Adding a frame to a painting on panel (such as the portrait featured above) is a great way to step it up. Many inexpensive artworks come on flat canvas panels or wood, which can look junky unframed. A frame with some heft adds to their visual presence and makes them look like a million bucks!

COMMON ROOKIE MISTAKES TO AVOID

CALM DOWN YOU'LL NEVER BE PERFECT

Scientists and moms everywhere agree: no one is perfect. You really need to accept this notion in order to be any good at interior design. You see, I used to be just like you, an insane nitpicking perfectionist who would stop at nothing to get what he wanted, no matter how many people I had to trample over, how many lives I had to ruin, how many species went extinct to keep me in the best furs money could buy. I did all the things I thought you were supposed to do, getting good grades and jumping through hoops to get into fancy colleges. And guess where it got me? NOWHERE. So one day I was all FUCK THIS I WANT TO PLAY WITH PILLOWS! So I got a job on a TV show about design and now I'm a famous designer writing a book. AND SO CAN YOU!

But first you have to just breathe, stop stressing about everything being perfect, and experiment. After all, design really is about finding the most aesthetically pleasing solution to the design conundrum at hand. And that solution usually comes as the result of throwing out a lot of ideas before you settle on one amazing one. A fun fact about being a designer is that it's our job to just throw out tons of ideas to our clients. And for the most part, clients just shit all over your ideas and hate all of them. It's one of the worst parts of being a designer, to be honest. You're just like, "Hey, why don't we do this?" and your client's like, "No, that's stupid I hate that" or "No, that's too expensive" or "No, that's too cheap."

You have to be willing to have your ideas shit upon if you are ever going to get anywhere design-wise. This means you have to just think of tons of design solutions, try them out, and if they don't work NO ONE DIED. Calm down. Making design progress involves being vulnerable. If you follow me on social media, you probably know being vulnerable is my thing. Maybe that's why I'm so good at design. I'm OK with putting it all out there, even if I know people might not like it. AND SO CAN YOU!

YOU'RE GOING TO MAKE MISTAKES SO DEAL WITH IT

When going into creating a design plan, remember: you're going to do it the wrong way and everyone will laugh at you. But that's part of the fun! Let's all agree that we're going to just enjoy ourselves, try new things, make mistakes, and eventually we'll all have the homes of our dreams.

HANGING A GODDAMN CHANDELIER TOO HIGH

Hanging a chandelier can be a tricky endeavor. The most common mistake people make is to hang it too high. You want to be able to interact with the chandelier, but you don't want it obstructing your view of the hot person sitting across the table from you. So you have to be strategic with figuring out the correct height. Luckily, there's a whole history of snobby interior designers clutching their pearls, ready to tell you exactly how to hang a fixture. The rules are as follows:

1. If you're hanging that shit in a hallway, give a bitch at least 7 feet of clearance.

2. If you're hanging the fixture above a breakfast nook, kitchen island, or dining table, give that motherfucker 30–34 inches between the bottom of the fixture and the tabletop.

3. If you're hanging a fixture above a bathtub, make sure there is at least 8 feet of clearance above the tub. If you don't, you'll die a rapid yet extremely painful death by electrocution. If you don't have space for that clearance, center that mofo in the room.

4. If you have a big-ass house with high-ass ceilings (more than 8 feet), add 3 inches per foot (of the ceiling height) to the height of the fixture. So if your ceiling is 10 feet high, your hanging height would be 36–40 inches.

5. Fixtures should be centered if they are over a dining table. Duh.

6. Same goes for beds or other room-defining furnishings.

PAINTING DARK SPACES WHITE

Many people think a surefire way to brighten up a dark space is to paint it white. Usually this just makes it look shadowy and dingy. Take this room, for example (at right). In person, the dark living room in the foreground reads dark and depressing. It's just begging for some pigment (even if it's just gray). The bright dining room in the background looks great painted white because it's bright. Avoid looking like a design rookie by avoiding this design faux-pas at all costs!

PUTTING SHIT ON A DIAGONAL

As a general rule, I hate it when anything rectangular is on a diagonal. Which means you should too. I don't have any real reasons, aside from the fact that this is a total goddamn fucking waste of space and makes no sense visually, but please don't do it. Sometimes people think it's cute to do this with a bed. NO. PUT THAT BED PERPENDICULAR TO THE WALL THE WAY GOD INTENDED. The only exception to this rule is if you're decorating some kind of campsite and you're trying to be irritatingly whimsical. Yes, if you're putting a bed in a yurt or another round room, you can get away with putting it diagonal because WHAT REALLY IS DIAGONAL IN THAT SITUATION ANYWAY?! Otherwise, BE A PERSON and put the bed perpendicular to the wall.

An aspect of a previous job I had was working with "influencer" clients to get press for our company. Guess what? Most of them were total pains in the ass and I hated working with them. One particularly awful one, who lied to my boss and told her I'd trashed her house (after I'd been on my hands and knees for hours cleaning her floors with my bare hands for a photo shoot) wanted everything for free and was generally a passive-aggressive nightmare to work with and totally rude and entitled even as I was going above the call of duty to literally open every single package that came to her house, dispose of all her garbage (do I look like a garbageman? OK don't answer that. But it wasn't my job to take out her trash), and do all sorts of handiwork that quite frankly I was beyond doing at that point. Oh, and she was also very rude and dismissive to all the workers and would talk about them in the third person in front of them, refusing to engage with them directly. The workers were Latino, she was white, and the whole dynamic pissed me off.

Whatever you do, respect people working in your house. It's Basic Humanity 101.

We were on a very tight deadline to get this project finished and gaining access to this space was a nightmare, so we had hours to install everything and a contractor who was basically doing this as a favor because no one wanted to pay him anything. Long story short, in the rush of everything the contractor hung the drapes too high. The annoying influencer was like, "Are those too high?" and

I was like, "Oh, no, that's fine" and ran out the door. My allegiance to my contractor, who had already been working for 15 hours, was much stronger than my allegiance to someone who lied, treated me like dirt, and had literally zero respect for any of my workers.

LET THIS BE A LESSON TO EVERYONE NOT TO CROSS ME (OR MY TEAM) OR I'LL HANG YOUR GODDAMN DRAPES TOO HIGH AND YOU'LL TOTALLY DESERVE IT.

Oh, and just so this isn't just me talking shit about an unnamed "influencer," the correct height for drapes is ⅛–½ inch off the floor. It can be very hard to get this exact, so don't be too hard on yourself if you're slightly off (drapery rods are very complicated beasts to hang). Once your drapes are up, if they are puddling on the floor or are more than a half inch off the ground, give yourself a quick, firm slap across the face and move on. If you try to rehang the rod, it'll just be too high or too low again. This is why you should never hang drapery rods yourself. It's better to have someone else do it so you can just blame them if the drapes are too high. You wouldn't have to get mad about it, but you also wouldn't have to live with the guilt of having completely fucked up the hanging of the drapes. As for height above windows, a team of scientists has decided that the drapery rod should be 4–12 inches above the top of the window. Do with that information what you will, but remember, they are scientists and are likely much smarter than you.

DOWN IN THE DUMPS: CREATING A POST-BREAKUP SPACE WHERE YOUR LIFE CAN STOP SUCKING

WAIT, WHAT HAPPENED? I'M ALONE NOW?

I've said it before (maybe even in this book) and I'll say it again, LIFE IS PAIN. But nothing is quite as painful as the guy you love more than anything being like, "SORRY DUDE I'M OVER YOU PLEASE LEAVE." I'm pretty well-versed at being dumped at this point. And while it's turned me into a weary, bitter, old garbage-troll who loves nothing better than screaming, "YOU'LL NEVER MAKE IT!" at young couples while they canoodle in public, one good thing has come from being the recipient of more than my fair share of rejection: I've learned a lot about building myself up so that the next time I get torn down it sucks slightly less.

GO, BE FREE! YOU ARE A WONDERSPIRIT

Something I learned during my first major breakup with Logan 1 (if you don't remember who that is, please go back to Chapter 1 AND PAY ATTENTION NEXT TIME) was that when someone dumps you the best thing to do is get out of town and explore. The year after we broke up, I was gone literally every weekend. Joshua Tree, Santa Barbara, New York, Ojai, Yosemite, Sonoma, Big Bear. I went all over California (I consider New York part of California, just mildly displaced and in the wrong time zone). Leaving town does something vital. It reminds you that your life, and the world you live in, isn't the whole

world. Stepping outside your regular life is the best way to get perspective on it.

BUT LIKE WHY? I'M SO CUTE AND FUN

When I was in college there were like ten gay guys and we all knew each other and were basically like brothers who hated each other. One day, a superhot engineering grad student (we'll call him Brandon) and I started dating and my friend Adam was like, "Oh my god you found the one cute gay guy to date. THANKS." Months later, I decided that I had to dump Brandon because I was twenty years old and he had yelled at me once while I was doing his dishes that I was using too much dish liquid. Anyway, I have a theory that he's still sitting at the restaurant where I dumped him, dumbfounded. "I AM THE CUTEST GODDAMN BOY AT THIS FUCKING SCHOOL," he must still be thinking, "HOW COULD I GET DUMPED I'M FUCKING GORGEOUS???"

In reality, Brandon is married and rich now (and I'm single, lived with my parents to write this, and slept in a room with a haunted mask named Brenda), so don't feel sorry for him. The reason I'm telling this story is to highlight that sometimes after you get dumped, you can go through a period of shock in which you truly cannot believe what has happened. This is a completely normal stage. And it's the best stage to start thinking about what you're going to do next and what sorts of fun design projects you can use to distract yourself from your abject misery.

OK FINE, I'MA GET WHAT I WANT

A wise woman once said, "SUCCESS IS THE BEST REVENGE HUNNY!" And it's true. But it turns out actual success is totally impossible to achieve so the best way for you to achieve revenge is to make yourself SEEM successful by giving yourself and your apartment way more glamour than you actually deserve. This section is all about how to design a revenge apartment that will not only make your ex jealous, it will also provide the framework for you to live the life you truly deserve. A life in which you come home, eat sushi, and cry on your (beautiful, custom) sofa every evening while polishing off an entire bottle of wine.

MAKING YOUR SPACE AS CODEPENDANT AS YOU ARE

OK ladiez, so this is how we're gonna do this. We are going to make your new, post-breakup space so gorgeous that you won't be sad anymore. "Tears? NO THANK YOU. I'm over that," you'll say to yourself as you laugh into a glass of champagne, your teeth glinting white in the sun, your skin a delectable sun-kissed color (even though you haven't been outside in three years). We are going to make a post-breakup home that will cause your ex to die instantaneously in a rage of envy.

YOU DO YOU

Having a space all to yourself is your chance to finally not give a shit about what your goddamn piece of shit ex-boyfriend—who is literal human garbage and should die in a fire—has to say about your decor choices. So have fun! I've always wanted an Art Deco-style curvaceous sofa, so I found a supercute vintage one for my new living room and was all, "HEY SOFA YOU'RE MY NEW BOYFRIEND."

COLOR ME HAPPY

Design can be a bridge that connects people and brings us all together. It's also a way to keep basic asshole guys from entering your life. That's why I painted my new bedroom pink. I wanted to make sure the next guy I date isn't so entangled in antiquated ideas of masculinity that he's freaked out by a Barbie pink bedroom. Make sure to make a few design choices that will frighten stupid people and keep them out of your life.

RAGE, AND MAKE SHIT YOURSELF

There's no better time to create art than when you feel outraged and hate the world. This is why I made my own artwork for my new living room. AND SO CAN YOU!

MAKE SPACE FOR GUESTS

If there's a guest bedroom, your friends will never leave AND YOU'LL NEVER HAVE TO BE ALONE WITH ALL THE DARKNESS THAT LIVES WITHIN YOU.

MAKE IT EASY TO ENTERTAIN

For your living space, opt for deep, comfortable seating. This will make all the fun Oscars parties and game nights way more enjoyable. And it will also make your friends less likely to abandon you. You know, the way your ex did.

CREATE A KITCHEN WHERE YOU CAN HAPPILY COOK BY YOURSELF

Have fond memories of cooking with your ex and having adorable food fights together and of feeling that life, for once, had meaning? Why not try to re-create that feeling by making sure your kitchen is outfitted with all the most glamorous finishes and cookware? I completely renovated the kitchen in my new place so it would be the perfect place to cook for friends. And for myself. While thinking about how life is ultimately meaningless.

CREATING A SPACE THAT REFLECTS YOUR AWFUL PERSONALITY

MILLENNIALS ARE DICKS

It surprises many of my fans and followers that, despite the fact that my face looks like a shriveled-up peach pit and I have the body of either an infant or a voluptuous eighty-seven-year-old woman, I am, in fact, a member of the millennial generation. One of the steadfast facts about us millennials is that we're fucking awful. We talk about our emotions all the time, we live with our parents forever, and we say "literally" all the time. So much in fact that they changed the definition of "literally" to not mean "literally" anymore. Like what the fuck is that? FUCK YOU MILLENNIALS AND FUCK YOU, SELF!

What happened to us? I think what made me terrible is that my twenties were a goddamn mess. I graduated from grad school into the Great Recession and basically couldn't get a job for years and years and years. This is actually when I started writing. Because as the old adage goes, "Those who cannot *do, write* about their feelings and fears on the Internet." I mean, I had nothing better to do, so I created a blog called *Orblogdo*. Typical self-absorbed millennial. I hate myself.

LOOK IN THE MIRROR, WHAT DO YOU SEE? IS IT GROSS?

Part of the reason I wrote this book is so that I could take you on a journey of self-discovery. So now we're gonna do a little quiz.

LOOK IN THE MIRROR. DO YOU SEE:

A. Someone who is attractive, successful, and smart.

B. Someone who is meh. Like not amazing but not terrible, to be honest.

C. Someone who is mildly vile.

D. Barf barf barf all over the mirror I suck and I'm ugly.

USE THIS FANCY DECODER TO FIND OUT WHAT YOUR ANSWER MEANS.

→ If you answered "A," you're a sociopath and have probably murdered dozens. You'll never truly love anyone because you're too obsessed with yourself. This is completely all your fault.

→ If you answered "B," you're not a total pyscho but you definitely killed someone in high school and somehow no one has found out about it yet. It's OK, I won't tell anyone, but you should take a moment to think about how you might be worse than you know.

→ Finally, someone who gets it. If you answered "C," you're fun at parties because you'll sit with me and talk shit about how lame the music is and how no one understands us.

→ You may have gone too far with the self-hatred, but it came from a good place. If you answered "D," be nicer to yourself. But not too much nicer, like 8 percent nicer.

Have you figured out how terrible you are yet? Phew! My job is done!

IT'S YOUR PARENTS' FAULT REALLY

One of my favorite undergraduate art professors taught me a very important secret to making yourself sound deep. "If people ask you what your art is about, just say 'unresolved parental conflict.'" And he's right. Not only is that a great defense for your bullshit painting, it's also a great defense for your horrible personality. I try to blame my parents for at least one thing on a daily basis. This lowers my stress level by taking the blame off myself and putting it where it belongs, on the people who created me and are therefore responsible for every single thing that happens in my life until the day I die. It's only fair.

ADDING YOUR DUMB PERSONALITY TO YOUR STUPID SPACE

It's likely that if you are reading this book you are a millennial, Generation Xer, or a baby boomer. And you all suck for different reasons. The baby boomers basically had a field day ruining the planet and created an economic boom that only they got to have fun with. Generation X was like, "YOU CAN'T SIT WITH US" and made millennials feel uncool because we were too young to understand grunge the first time (which is probably why we brought it back). And yeah, millennials are annoying as fuck because we won't shut up ever. I don't even know what comes after millennials and I don't want to know. I'm assuming it's just heads on skateboards attached to smartphones that communicate with each other solely through emoji Morse code.

Even knowing how terrible we are, we still want to see ourselves reflected in our home spaces. But how do you do that? For me, adding little hints of myself, my family, and places important to me makes my space feel homier. Here's a few ways I like to add hints of personality in a space without being one of those couples that has their wedding photos and nothing else hanging all over their homes (you know who you are).

Display Personal Photos in an Unconventional Way

It may come as a shock to many of you that we can still print photographs. There are plenty of companies out there willing to take those digital images off your phone and turn them into actual, printed photographs. It feels like a miracle, but it's something they used to do all the time in the olden days. They'd snap a pic, wait 6–10 weeks for it to be developed, and then when the collection of photographic prints arrived, it would be a reason for the whole town to rejoice. Families would sit around together sipping cups of hot cocoa, looking over the photos, and remembering together. Consider tossing a number of printed photos in a shallow tray on your coffee table, as in the image above.

Faces Are Literally the Easiest Way to Insert Personality into Your Home

I don't know where this fascination came from, but I love anything with a face on it. That's why I filled my bedroom with this terrifying collection of faces. To some people, it's creepy. To me, it's built-in friends. Like every time I go in there it's like, OH THANK GOD YOU'RE HERE I WAS SO ALONE. But seriously folks, if you're looking to insert a little more personality into your home, accessories with faces is the best place to start. And if you can't find them, just make them yourself. I took a boring-ass candle and painted a frownie on it. Just a LITTLE bit of paint added A LOT of personality.

Don't Plaster Family Photos All Over the Living Room Even Though That Totally Seems Like the Right Thing to Do

Hallways are the best place to display family photographs. That way, as you pass through your home you can take

a minute to remember all the fun stuff your family does together when you're not fighting at the dinner table. Displaying family photos in places where you're bound to sit for a while (like a living room) is truly psychotic and tells your guest, "YOU'RE GONNA LOOK AT ME. YOU'RE GONNA FUCKIN' LOOK AT ME FOR AS LONG AS I WANT YOU TO AND THERE'S NOTHING YOU CAN DO ABOUT IT. YOU'RE STUCK HERE NOW AS MY PRISONER AND AIN'T NO ONE COMIN' TO HELP YOU! NOT EVER!!!"

Family Heirlooms, Family Influences

My mom grew up in Japan and a lot of her imagination still stems from that experience. She has passed down not only Japanese antiques to me, but a love for the Japanese aesthetic and culture. Displaying these items, such as the *tansu* (in my guest bedroom, above), is a way for me to subtly add bits of family history to my home. AND SO CAN YOU!

You Can Have Family Photos in Common Areas If They're Chic and You Mix Them with Other Accessories

People often comment, "You don't have any family photos in your house." Which is a lie. I have them. They're just not giant and thrust up into your face. I like to keep family photos in albums and when they're on display I like them to have something distinctive about them. I broke my own rule by putting a family photo on the mantel. But it's a retro-looking family photo encased in Lucite, so it's hip and cool and not gross. See? You can break rules if you do it with style! I guess what I'm saying here is make it personal BUT KEEP IT ELEGANT.

I MEAN, WHAT IS "LIFE" REALLY?

At the risk of sounding totally philosophical and supersmart, like what is life or whatever? For me, even though I am an awful person and a tirelessly self-absorbed millennial, what makes life fun is thinking about memories with my family and friends. So adding decor that reminds me of these times is important to me. I just try to do it in a way that's not too cloying and cute.

Also, don't be one of those people who displays giant wedding photos all over their living room and the rest of the house. You can have like one in the hallway but that's it. The rest should be in an album. And if your friends don't wanna look at that album, they're probably sociopaths. I never understood people who don't care about looking at family photos. It's like the first thing I want to see when I walk into someone's house. So if you try to show someone your wedding album and they get bored, remove them from your life immediately. Just remember, wedding photos are not decor, they're for albums. Unless Annie Leibovitz shot your wedding and it took place on a glacier and you wore a Björk swan dress. Then maybe that can go in the living room. Otherwise no way, no ma'am! Sorry.

Collect Things Over Time

There's no better way to insert your personality into your space than to fill it with things that strike your fancy. So keeping your eyes open for objects that speak to you as you travel is the best way to make your space a true reflection of you. My friends always point out objects in my home and say, "OMG that's so you!" It's hard to say why something reflects who I am, but the fact that I was attracted to it probably means something. Take the three blind mice prop in this shelving. I bought that and was immediately told, "That's so you." I have no idea why, it just is. Maybe because, like me, it's adorable, quirky, partially broken, and old? No one can really put a finger on what makes you YOU but when you see it, you know it. So keep looking around for accessories that call your name and when you see them, snatch them up!

IF YOUR KIDS ARE BRATS IT'S PROBABLY YOUR FAULT FOR NOT MAKING THEIR ROOMS CUTE ENOUGH

CHILDREN ARE FUCKING AWFUL I KNOW BECAUSE I WAS ONE

In Yosemite National Park where I grew up there are really only two acceptable restaurants. One is the dining room at the Ahwahnee Hotel and the other is a restaurant at the Yosemite Valley Lodge called the Mountain Room. When I was little, my parents used to go on dates to these places (or the famed Erna's Elderberry House in nearby Oakhurst if they were feeling particularly fancy). While I have no idea how these dates went, I have strong memories of these evenings for one reason and one reason alone: TERROR.

I'm the youngest of three children and my parents would always leave my older brother, Miguel (surprise! we're kinda Latino!) to babysit my sister, Elisa, and me. And by "babysit," I basically mean Miguel spent hours torturing us. A favorite trick was to convince us (god we were such dumb idiots) to make a house out of sofa cushions and get inside. Then he'd jump on top of it and smash us like pancakes and chase us through the house. When Miguel got older my parents got him a BB gun, which he loved doing target practice with. The targets? Elisa and me. My sister and I were like Mole People, trapped in a house with a sadistic torturer. That is until my sister turned into a torturer as well and then I was left as the lone victim of not one, but two psychopaths.

When my siblings got older, like high school age, and started smoking pot and acting like general badasses while I was still a dorky goody-two-shoes (sidenote: I never exited this phase UNTIL THE WRITING OF THIS BOOK WHEN I LEARNED HOW TO USE CURSE WORDS AND BECAME TOTALLY EDGY AND COOL), they used to get high and make me get them snacks. I'd be like, "WHY ARE THEY SO HUNGRY?" I was pretty dense and got all my info about what families were like from TGIF and *My So-Called Life*. So yeah, my siblings were pretty much buttholes until they left for college, and then I was all alone to finally live the life I'd always been meant to live. The life of an only child.

I bring all this up not to bore you with my childhood stories, but to remind you of one important fact: CHILDREN ARE THE GODDAMN WORST. We live in a culture in which we idealize kids and like to think of them as little angels. Yes, children are precious and should be protected as long as possible from the harsh realities of adult victimhood, but they are by no means innocent. DO YOU EVEN REMEMBER BEING A KID?

One time when I was five, I was riding my bike and a kid came up and was like, "YOU HAVE AIDS." I had no idea what that even meant. I think of all kids I was probably the only sweet/innocent one, which is why I grew up to have way too many feelings. I guess those AIDS-pointing kids had probably seen something about Magic Johnson, whose HIV status had recently come out. Children are a lot more complex than we give them credit for. And part of that complexity is that they have the ability to be incredibly cruel and awful to each other. Don't go out and post-birth abort your babies or anything, just stop pretending children are angels. They're more like demons in cherub costumes. BEWARE OF THEIR TRICKERY AND MALICIOUS INTENTIONS.

DO YOU HATE YOUR CHILDREN?

Before we get to the nitty-gritty of your problems, we need to talk about whether or not you completely hate your kids. Does your skin crawl when little Sally comes up behind you and shrieks, "MOMMY BUY ME THIS HOT DOG!" Do you feel like stabbing yourself in the inner ear when little Bobby saunters into the room and bellows, "MOMMEEEEE GIMME UR PHONE I WANT TO PLAY POKÉMON HO" (Pokémon Ho is a new prostitution-themed version of the classic PokémonGo game, updated for today's completely messed-up generation of kids who grew up way too fast because INTERNET).

For Mother's/Father's Day did your kid give you a drawing of an owl they made THAT TOTALLY DIDN'T EVEN LOOK LIKE A FUCKING OWL EVEN THOUGH THEY'VE BEEN IN PRIVATE ART LESSONS FOR THREE YEARS? Are your kids ever like, "DADDY I'M HUNGRY!" And you're like, "WHAT ABOUT ME!?! I'm hungry too! Why don't YOU make ME a pizza???" The worst thing about kids is they always think about their needs and never about yours. It's really selfish if you think about it.

I'm not trying to dis on your kids. Allz I'm saying is that it's OK if you hate your kids and think they're annoying. Everyone else does, too.

SERIOUSLY, ARE THEY DEMONS?

Sometimes, when your children are screaming like the possessed girl in *The Exorcist*, it's hard to remember why you did this in the first place. "Why," you ask yourself, "WHY DID I GROW THIS DEMON INSIDE ME AND LET IT VIOLENTLY EXPLODE OUT ME!?!" Then they'll do something cute and say, "I love you Mommy!" DO NOT FALL FOR THIS. This is a specific ploy to keep you from giving them up for adoption, children have stronger survival instincts than the rest of us. View your children in much the same way you viewed your archenemies from high school. Be like, "HEY BECKY HOW ARE U LOVE U!!!" But really be thinking, "If you make one false move, you're dead, Becky."

EVERYTHING IS YOUR FAULT

When contemplating the demonhood of your children, it's important to remember that everything they are is your fault and a direct result of you fucking them up. This is why it's up to you to exorcize the demons within them by doing your best to make them less garbage-y than they currently are. There is only one way to do this. The only way to make your kids stop being assholes is to make their bedrooms so gorgeous it's literally impossible for them to keep being such dicks.

DESIGN THE PAIN AWAY

"But how!?!" you ask. "How can I make my children stop being buttholes with design?" I'll tell you, this is going to

be way easier than you thought! The thing is, kids are way better at being emotionally manipulative than adults are, but somehow they're also way dumber. So you don't really have to do that much to trick them into thinking their room is the most amazing bedroom any kid has ever had. Here are a few design tips that will help take your kids' demon level from a 10 to a 4.

Kids Love Stickers So Put Them on Their Walls

Stickers for the wall are called decals and they're perfect for families too lazy or afraid to paint their walls. Added bonus: the more time your kids spend peeling these stickers off the wall, the less time they spend plotting their anarchic takeover of your household and/or torturing their hamster.

Remind Them You Control the Money by Painting Things Gold

One way to ensure your kids don't kill you is to remind them that if you are dead they'll have no way to access your bank account. Painting furniture gold makes them think of golden coins (which were used as currency in the olden days) and that reminds them of how precarious their financial situation would be if they killed you. PROBLEM SOLVED!

Someday Your Children Will Run Away and Take Their Furniture with Them, Make Sure the Furniture Is Grown Up and Cool Enough to Look Good in Their Santa Cruz Apartment

Someday, after you've clothed, fed, and loved your kids for years and years, they'll leave you all alone. Unless

they're me, in which case they'll live with you well into their thirties. Make sure their furniture makes sense for their new bohemian lifestyle by choosing classic pieces in mid-century styles.

Oversize Stuffed Animals Make Totally Cute Decor Accents

A team of researchers found that children whose parents bought them too many giant stuffed animals were 80 percent less likely to secretly shoot up heroin in their bedrooms than children of parents who bought them zero giant stuffed animals. Thus, it's pretty obvious that you should be buying the fuck out of some giant stuffed animals.

Try to Subconsciously Control Their Minds by Organizing Their Rooms

One thing that all children are plagued with is a general desire for their rooms to look like they were just hit by a massive tornado. This is because all children are anarchists and don't believe in the patriarchal structure they've been born into. This is my favorite thing about kids, to be honest. But you must suppress it as much as you can, because

accepting them as anarchists means accepting their busted-ass rooms. Organize their toys into bins and bookcases so everything stays orderly and to avoid an anarchist uprising in your own home.

Be Playful with Paint

A kid's room is the perfect place to go crazy with paint colors and nontraditional wall treatments. For this beach-inspired kid's room (above), I did a Seussian wave pattern and dual-tone color blocking to create an underwater oasis fit for mermaid royalty. This effect is relatively easy to achieve. Start by painting the top of the room one color, then add the second color (block off the top half with blue painter's tape to give yourself a guide of where to stop). Then use a pencil to draw your wave pattern and use small artist paintbrushes to fill in the wave shapes.

Go Crazy with Color

Kids spend most of their time alone in their bedrooms thinking about how they'd get by if they murdered you in your sleep. Using a saturated color palette elevates their serotonin levels, thereby distracting them from their urge to stab you while you're snoozing. EVERYONE WINS!

Rugs Not Drugs

The science on whether having a rug actually prevents kids from doing drugs is inconclusive; I just wanted to include that as a tip. Sorry. But as I've said before, rugs help define a space and provide the softness and texture that just might keep your little one from becoming a hard-core drug addict when she grows up.

CRISIS OF MASCULINITY: DESIGNING FOR DUDES

PEOPLE ALWAYS ASK ME HOW DO I DO IT?

You know, people always ask me, "Can you give me some tips on designing a space that dudes would be into? I'm trying to make my apartment a place that both my boyfriend and I can enjoy!" And I'm like, "Ma'am, I'm literally wearing a tutu right now, standing inside a giant human-size replica of a Glitter Beach Barbie box. What on EARTH makes you think I'd know anything about masculine design?" At which point the annoying lady asking me this question clutches her pearls, rips them from her throat, and storms off.

Peeps be obsessed with thinking there are magic tricks to designing for guys. I don't know why they think this, but it makes everyone feel better. Sometimes, I think all people (even FEMINISTS) feel comforted fixating on the stereotypical differences between men and women. It makes them feel like there is order in the world and that they understand their role on earth a bit better. But I mean, honestly, designing things in a gender-specific way is simplistic and basic and all the other things none of us want to be. But we do it anyway. Because defined gender differences make us feel like there is world order. And feeling like there is order in the world makes us feel more in control and feeling more in control makes us feel like we aren't just tiny worthless specks sitting on a rock flying around in space that could be obliterated by an asteroid at any moment causing the immediate extinction of humanity. MMMMMMKAY?

So given that there is no reality and that gender is just a construct we've created to make ourselves feel like the world isn't 100 percent chaos, LET'S TALK ABOUT DUDE BRO MASC DESIGN! I have worked with many a bachelor client, so I have many Tips-N-Tricks to share with you about

the topic. So look into my man-eyes, and let me take you on a journey of exploration. A journey into decor POUR HOMME. A MAN JOURNEY.

WHAT'S THE DIFFERENCE BETWEEN A DUDE, A BRO, AND A BRAH?

Before we discuss anything else, I have a confession to make. Are you sitting down? This one is going to be a lot for you to take and you might need a cool, refreshing glass of water once I've told you. So go ahead, go grab yourself a nice tall glass of water. Did you get it? Are you sitting down? OK, here goes nothing.

I'M GAY!!!

I'm sorry. I had to tell you at some point. I hope you're not too shocked and that you're starting to calm down by now. I'd always dreamed you'd find this out by reading it on the cover of *People* magazine with the title "YEP! I'm Gay!" But alas, they never showed any interest in the repeated coming-out stories I pitched to them (each one including a superelaborate photo series!). It really angers me because those of us who were never closeted really miss out on press opportunities. I came out when I was fourteen, so I never got the chance to use my fun gay coming-out story to whore myself out to the media and further my career, which is really bullshit if you think about it. FUCK YOU WORLD. Just let me have my goddamn coming-out story! PAY ATTENTION TO ME AND MY GAY FACE!

Wait, I lost my train of thought. Why are we talking about me being gay in a section about dude design? Oh yeah, because I have no idea what the deal with straight male culture is. All of my tips about dude design will be based on my very slim understanding of masculinity, which

I see solely through the tiny gay lens through which I view everything. Here are some terms that I've learned from being a Gay:

MASC

This means you wear baseball hats and tank tops and like to talk about sports even though it's unlikely that you play them. If you're on a gay Internet dating site, saying that you're looking for "masc" guys means you are looking for guys who are either still closeted or who spend their time mimicking straight men from action movies in order not to look like supergay lady faces when they go on dates. The community of men who are into masc culture refer to each other and are collectively known as MASC4MASC.

CHILL

While not a specifically masculine term, "chill" has been co-opted by the Masc4Masc community to be code for "not sissygay." When a gay man says he wants to do something chill, he means he wants to drink beer and act straight with you while he talks a lot about how much he loves his family while secretly being overwhelmed with the fear that his lisp might come out if he drinks too much.

BRO

A bro is an asshole guy/stockbroker/hedge fund dickhead who was once in a fraternity and/or wanted to be in one. He likes to tell you about indie bands but it's just always bands he learned about at Coachella with his dude posse. Bros are usually straight. Gay bros are a step above MASC4MASC Gays, and usually slightly nicer and less worried about their ladylike hand gestures and thin, delicate lady fingers.

MAN CAVE

This is basically a sewing room but for a man. The room is so inherently feminine that it's been given a masculine name to counterbalance the *vaginality* of everything, which can threaten members of the Male Community. Usually there's a TV in here where men can watch "the sports" but mostly they watch *Real Housewives* when no one is looking.

WHAT IS MASC?

MASC is really just a feeling, a way of describing raw masculinity. But for us non-MASC people out there, I have a simple trick for understanding MASC. Whenever someone uses the word "MASC," just replace it with "mask." MASC is a mask that men can wear to feel good about themselves. It's kind of like how sometimes ladies put on diamonds and fancy lingerie and high heels to cook dinner for their lazy disgusting straight husbands (ladies do that, right?). MASC is the lingerie that men put on to feel attractive to themselves and others. But mostly to themselves. MASC is a mask, but a mask is not MASC. Wearing a costume, especially a mask, is most certainly not considered masculine in the Male Community.

MASC is really just a feeling. And that feeling is "If I don't dress and act this way, I could be ostracized. And if I'm ostracized how will I use my male privilege to boss other people around?"

ARE BOY HOUSES DIFFERENT FROM LADYHOUSES?

Now that we have defined the terms involved in the current crisis of male gender identity, we can move onto talking about how this affects the design of the dwellings in which this species make their homes. So what makes a home appropriate for a Dude, a Bro, or a MASC4MASC man? Well, I'll tell you.

MINIMALISM

Ever notice how every super-MASC villain in a movie lives in a superminimal high-rise Manhattan apartment (even if the movie takes place in Kentucky)? That's no coincidence. It's a scientific fact that masculine men enjoy living in modern, minimal homes. Especially sociopaths hell-bent on murdering everyone. Since 79 percent of men are sociopaths, you can guess that the guy in your life will LOVE a modern, minimal design.

NO COLOR OK MAYBE SOME BLUE

Members of the Male Community tend to be afraid of color. I'm not entirely sure why, perhaps it relates back to that time they wore pink in kindergarten and were perceived as non-MASC by all the other MASC bro kindergarten brahs. One color that is acceptable to most dudes is blue. This is because they've been stereotyped and pigeonholed their whole lives, led to believe the only color they should like is blue. And thank god, to be honest, because blue is a great color. OR MAYBE I ONLY THINK THAT BECAUSE I'VE BEEN CONDITIONED TO THINK THAT BECAUSE OF MY GENDER.

BLACK-AND-WHITE HORSE PHOTOS

This is a specific one, but if you're designing a space for a man, you can bet he wants a giant black-and-white photograph of a horse incorporated into the design. Scientists are conflicted as to why this is, but most believe it has something to do with members of the Male Community either being attracted to the horse or wanting to identify as the horse.

INDUSTRIAL

Your man wants to believe he's a steelworker, even if his job is cushier than first class on Emirates airline. Therefore, he just LOVES an industrial accent. Anything made from raw metal makes members of the Male Community go nuts!

WOOD

Want to impress a Dude? Design him a room full of wood. Dudes love saying the words "oak," "reclaimed," and "salvaged." In fact, studies have shown that men who hear the word "wood" within six hours of bedtime are 54 percent more likely to initiate an intimate encounter.

MID-CENTURY ANYTHING

If there's anything men love more than being stylish, it's mansplaining design history to other people. Therefore, mid-century furniture is their favorite kind of furniture. This type of furniture has the combined benefit of being warm and having clean, masculine lines. It also makes guys think of *Mad Men*, a show they enjoy because it has the word "Men" in the title. If you're on a date with a man and the

conversation dies down, ask him about his mid-century coffee table. He'll talk for hours and hours about how it's by Milo Baughman. He'll talk so long you won't even have to say anything. You can just sit there objectifying him. And when he stops talking, just say, "Oh, I never knew that!" Men love that response!

LEATHER

Men love leather because it is weathered, aged, and masculine like the skin of their leader, Clint Eastwood.

ANYTHING GRAFFITI-INSPIRED

Dudes are afraid of art because they think being creative is feminine, but the one acceptable art form they're not ashamed to admit they like is graffiti. Graffiti makes them think of gangs tagging shit and thinking about gangsters makes them feel like they are cool, tough gang members.

SPORTS-RELATED ACCESSORIES

Items like surfboards and skateboards affirm a man's masculinity, even if they never use them. A bonus for design lovers: they actually make great design accessories because of their size and shape. Try using one in your home to butch it up!

BAR

Men love a bar. It reminds them of James Bond. Which reminds them that inside all of them is a dashing superhero.

BIG NO-NO'S FOR YOUR BIG BOY

There are certain things that men, whether they be members of the Dude, Bro, MASC4MASC, or simply of the Male Community cannot stand. I'll list them for you here so you can avoid being insensitive to their very specific masculine needs.

SISAL RUGS

I don't know why, but for some reason guys don't like these. If you try to get a man to walk barefoot on a sisal rug he'll immediately start wailing audibly and complaining about how the "ruggy scratchy my toesies." It's an

unexplained phenomenon, but researchers believe that the male epidermis lacks a protective barrier present in members of the much more resilient Female Community.

LINEN SHEETS

As with sisal rugs, a shocking 98 percent of members of the Male Community complain of discomfort when using linen sheets. This is a strange and upsetting percentage, as the stereotypical MASC ideal is strong and tough. But a man's dainty skin is no match for the sharp, razorlike fibers of a linen sheet. Protect the precious men in your life from these punishing textiles at all costs!

ACCESSORIES

Men have an innate fear of clutter and lady objects. Thus, they hate accessories. Strangely, if you ask them to show you a picture of a house they like, it'll be full of accessories. Men are stupid idiots. I've had countless male clients and most of them have refused to let me accessorize their homes. Except gay guys, who are like regular men but better because they GET IT.

HOMME LIFE

What separates humans from wild animals? Mosty our ability to do fancy domestic things. It may seem daunting to arrange flowers or plan the perfect cocktail party, but these things are literally the easiest things on earth. The previous chapters helped you figure out how to transform your home's interior from awful to amazing. This chapter is all about the fun things you can do in your new glamorous space. As a lifelong shut-in who hates going outside, I'm an expert in home life. Follow along with me as I teach you everything you'll ever need to know about how to get the most out of your time at home and how to be the best host ever (even to guests you hate!).

HOW TO MAKE NON-GARBAGEY FLOWER ARRANGEMENTS

WOULD YOU LIKE IT IF SOMEONE CUT OFF YOUR ARMS AND SOLD THEM SO PEOPLE COULD SHOVE THEM INTO VASES?

Before we start chatting about flower arrangements and the dos and don'ts involved, we should chat a little bit about how weird it is that we display flowers in our homes. I've never really been a fan of cut flowers because they're already dead when you get them. What's romantic about getting a bunch of flowers that are already decaying, reminding us all of our own mortality? Also, they're a pain in the ass to take care of. If you don't change the water every day they start smelling immediately like swamp mold.

I'm not a huge fan of flowers for a lot of reasons. Mainly, they are shipped all over the world and seem like a huge waste of fossil fuel for something that's just going to sit there reminding you that you yourself are also slowly rotting. Think about how weird it would be if someone came up to you and was like, "HEY CAN I CHOP OFF YOUR ARM SO THESE GIANTS CAN STICK IT IN A VASE AND STARE AT IT ALL DAY?" You'd be weirded out, right? I think flowers have every right to be pissed that you think it's perfectly OK to rip their arms off and display them in your home. You're pretty sick if you think about it.

WHY PEOPLE LOVE FLOWERS EVEN THOUGH THEY'RE DEAD

OK, so even though I've explained why I think flowers represent everything that's wrong with the world, I understand why people like them. Here's a list that shows how flowers can help spruce up your home:

1. They make your space look way fancier than it really is.

2. If you can't keep plants alive because you have a black thumb, flowers are a good way to bring some life indoors.

3. If you screwed up and forgot to include enough color in your design plan, they're a great way to bring color into a room.

4. Flowers sometimes smell good, so if your house smells gross they'll help cover up that vile odor.

5. Flowers remind people of spring, and spring reminds people of youth and rejuvenation, and that makes them feel fresh and youthful. Which is ironic because flowers are dead and slowly getting more rotten every second.

YOU KILLED THESE FLOWERS, THIS IS THE LEAST YOU COULD DO

OK, so you personally murdered these plants just so you could bring them inside and watch them slowly die. CONGRATULATIONS! The following is the LEAST you could do to pay respect to the lives you so ruthlessly cut short:

1. Trim them immediately, at a 45-degree angle.
2. Put them in water immediately. Not warm water, not cold water, just room temperature water.
3. Once you've put them in a vase, change their water every day.

MAKING FLOWER ARRANGEMENTS IS POSSIBLE, BUT YOU PROBABLY CAN'T DO IT

Curating a pretty combination of flowers is known as "Flower Arranging." Flower arranging dates back centuries, and through the ages there have been countless flower arranging artists with a natural talent for mixing and matching flowers to create beautiful compositions. I'm here to tell you something potentially tragic. It's very unlikely that you're one of these geniuses. You see, when most of us try to mix different flower varieties together to make beautiful arrangements, it ends up looking like someone barfed into a vase. I'm sure this is probably very difficult for you to hear, but it's the truth. Most people, myself included, are cursed to only be able to make superhideous flower arrangements. It's not your fault, we're just born this way. But there is a solution and I'm going to share it below.

The solution is to simply use one flower variety per vase. This way, the design of your arrangement doesn't get too chaotic and will look less like barf. It's hard enough to arrange even one species of flower in a way that is attractive. Now imagine trying to arrange multiple varieties so they don't look like projectile vomit. IT'S IMPOSSIBLE. This is why florists exist. They are the only ones in our culture capable of mixing flower varieties

and creating something beautiful. The rest of us should just stick to one type of flower per vase, OR RISK CREATING AN ARRANGEMENT THAT BRINGS SHAME UPON OUR FAMILIES.

THROW THAT NASTY VASE AWAY

While florists are geniuses at creating beautiful flower arrangements, for some reason they are fucking terrible at choosing vases that aren't totally ugly. For this reason, it is imperative that you immediately throw away the vase your arrangement comes in and put the arrangement in a pretty vase you bought yourself. I don't know why this is, it's just a scientific fact that all florist-supplied vases are extremely ugly. If you're a mom, especially my mom, you'll have the urge to save the vase, regardless of how ugly it is. But no one wants that ugly, red frosted-glass vase. So you can just recycle it and move on. To all the moms out there who may have saved florist vases, throw them away. Maureen, I'm talking to you. You don't need all those vases you're keeping in the garage. I PROMISE.

RIGHT VASE, WRONG TIME

Now that we've discussed all the important matters surrounding floral arranging,
let's talk about some dos and don'ts.

DO: Allow certain plants (like palm fronds) to stand on their own. They're intricate enough to put in a vase all alone.

DO: Pair distinctive vases with distinctive foliage that accentuates their style (like this cute lady vase with that pink flower-hair).

DO: Make sure you have enough plants to fill out the whole vase and make it look full.

DON'T: Forget to trim leaves off the lower portion of a stem and just shove them in the water.

DON'T: Use a vase that's way out of scale with the length of your stems (like this insane Bells of Ireland in a tiny-ass vase situation).

DON'T: Put a tiny, short flower in a tall/giant vase.

HOW TO THROW A MAJOR RAGER

WHY WE MUST RAGE

Through the ages, one thing has never changed. Collectively, the human culture has recognized one need above all others: OUR NEED TO RAGE. While food, shelter, love, and fulfillment rank high on our list of priorities, researchers have found that the number-one priority of all people surveyed was the desire to rage at parties and really crush it, regardless of the physical or mental repercussions of RAGING AS HARD AS HUMANLY POSSIBLE.

While it's important to party, many people feel daunted by the task of hosting. But there comes a time where it's our turn to host and we cannot shirk that duty. As party people, we must contribute to the party community by hosting a fete from time to time. But you don't have to lose your goddamn mind trying to host a complicated party. There are many tricks to making your party seem way more glam than it actually is. If you stick around, I'll teach them to you.

CREATING A SUPEREXCLUSIVE INVITE LIST

When creating a guest list for the PERFECT PARTY, many factors come into consideration. In figuring out who you should invite, keep the following in mind:

1. Which of my friends have wronged me in the past 12–16 months?

2. Have any of the potential guests questioned my dignity or done anything that might have caused my social media following to dwindle?

3. Do any of these guests pose a professional, romantic, or emotional threat to me?

4. Will this guest's presence create any drama at the party?

5. Will it be good drama or bad drama?

6. Where did this potential guest's great grandfather go to college?

TURN THAT SMILE UPSIDE DOWN!

For an added injection of FUN, I like to make my own outfits for a party. For this party, I created a cozy costume out of what are essentially pajamas. How'd I make these non-pajamas? By painting a frown on them. Turns out painting a frown on your chest makes everyone happy. I don't know why. 100 percent of the people I surveyed about my party costume were either totally confused by it or completely loved it. However, those who were confused were also amused so I increased the happiness factor by 200 percent just by wearing this stupid outfit.

LET'S FACE IT, WE GONNA LOSE OUR MINDZ

When planning a party, it's important to make sure you're making provisions for how completely destroyed you are going to get. Therefore, I find Fridays and Saturdays the best days to host a cocktail party. You need a full day of wallowing and cleanup following a decent party. So don't make plans to have lunch with your mom the day after a party or go to an art museum. Trust me, you're just gonna wanna hang out and chill at home while yelling at your housekeeper to clean up faster (this is even more taxing if you're your own housekeeper, as you'll be relentlessly demanding of yourself).

SET THE SCENE, THEN MAKE A SCENE!

One of the key ingredients to a successful party is the space in which it takes place. One thing many people overlook is that their home's everyday setup might not be party appropriate. Most of the time, you're going to need to rearrange your space so it's more amenable to the flow of the party. This means clearing out more space for people to congregate, moving chairs away from tables and into seating areas, and perhaps even hiding some of your furniture in the garage so there's enough space for all your guests. Think of your guests as less-important pieces of furniture. They're gonna take up space. So you might need to get rid of some furniture to make space for your guests.

The name of the game with party organizing is clearing out, making space for what happens at a party. What happens at parties? Mostly people grab a drink, then set it down, then forget which drink is theirs and go get another drink. They repeat this all night until there's no glasses left, then everyone is too drunk to care that they're just picking up random glasses and drinking from them and that's why all your friends have herpes now. But that's their problem. Your problem is making sure they have enough space to put their glasses, which may mean clearing away some of your tabletop accessories and putting out a variety of coasters so they don't ruin your furniture, which is more important than your friends are.

One thing that drives me crazy is people in the kitchen, so I always try to put the drinks anywhere but the kitchen. Even with all the drinks outside, people will still congregate in the kitchen, but the crowd will be significantly smaller. Note to party guests: spend as little time in the kitchen as possible. There's nothing more annoying than hosting a party and having eight hundred people in your kitchen when you're trying to get a goddamn pitcher of booze to refill the drink dispenser and everyone's just sitting there in your way laughing their heads off like the boy-donkeys in that scary scene in *Pinocchio*. If you need something in the kitchen, grab it, then run out of there as fast as possible. Anything else is tacky and rude. GET OUT OF MY KITCHEN.

CAREFREE COCKTAILS

Parties are meant to be enjoyed, so it's important to prep as much as you can beforehand so when your guests show up you can just LOL and ROFL with them. This is why I like to premake the specialty cocktails and serve them in handy drink dispensers. You can even make extra cocktails and store them in pitchers in the refrigerator so that when your out-of-control alcoholic guests drink the entire contents of the drink dispenser you can easily refill it. These cocktail recipes are pretty simple to make.

SIMPLE SPARKLING SPIKED LEMONADE

Juice of 2 lemons, sparkling pink lemonade, and vodka. Mix together until you can just taste the vodka but its flavor isn't too strong. Garnish with rosemary sprigs.

TEQUILA LIMEADE

Juice of 4–6 limes, limeade, and tequila. Mix together until you can just taste the tequila but its flavor isn't too strong. Garnish with fresh mint.

I like to add garnishes to these drinks because it makes them look, feel, and smell like specialty cocktails even though they're just basically juice and booze. Most people are idiots and can't tell the difference between this and something a handlebar mustached "artisanal cocktail craftsperson" might create.

KEEP THE FOOD AND BEV AS BASIC AS YOUR FRIENDS

I like to keep things simple for myself by setting boundaries. For this party, I did a few cocktails and then served rosé. Yes, it would have been nice to have a full bar with every kind of booze available. But it would also have been nice to be born with a megatrust fund and to not have to work for my money, and you don't see me complaining! If you're trying to host a party without breaking the bank, choose just a few drinks/snacks to offer and let anyone who asks know. Say something like, "We're gonna have tequila, vodka, and rosé, so if you want something else bring it!" True friends don't mind. Also, I think because I live in L.A. and I'm used to every single person I know having some weird diet where they can only eat/drink very specific things, I've just given up on thinking I'll be able to have something for everyone. You could spend the family fortune buying every mixer/booze known to man and someone would show up and be all, "Oh, I'm on this new diet where I only drink Slurpee remnant and tequila effervescence." It's literally impossible to please everyone, so just make sure you've got the basics and let people know if they want something else they can bring it.

IMPRESS YOUR FRIENDS WITH REAL GLASS!

Small details can completely change the feel of a party. I'm a huge proponent of using reusable dishes at parties. And the same goes for glassware. Yes, it's a pain in the ass to deal with, but it changes the look and feel of your party, making it feel more grown-up and gorgeous. And these cocktail glasses can be inexpensively sourced at restaurant supply stores.

FANCY SNACKS THAT WON'T BREAK THE BANK

Determining the start time for your party is a difficult balancing act. If you start too early, people will expect dinner. If you put the start time too late, people will show up at 4 a.m. in the year 2075. OMG, what if you're reading

this book in the year 2075? How's the future? Are you a head on a skateboard who communicates exclusively through emoji Morse code? HAS THE APOCALYPSE HAPPENED YET? Anyway, it's key to start a party after dinnertime but before it gets so late that people will think it's a late-night crazy party. I think any time between 8:07 p.m. and 9:13 p.m. is a good time to start a party. And yes, I like to give start times that specific. I find that if I put the start time at a superweird/random time people will actually show up near that time. Mostly to be funny. They'll be like, "Well it's 8:09 but I'm almost on time!" and you'll just laugh knowing that you mind-controlled them into not showing up at 10 p.m. by using a random/specific start time.

ADULTS LIKE TOYS

It might seem silly to buy toys for full-on grown-ups, but a fun party favor can really liven up a party. I bought glow sticks and glow balloons for this party and people lost their minds playing with them. It reminded them of raves they'd gone to in 1996, which made them nostalgic for being six years old. Adding in a few playful party favors is a fun way to tell your guests, "Hey, I may look like Jessica Tandy in *Cocoon*, but I can still party with the best of them!"

WHAT TO DO WHEN GUESTS GET OUT OF ORDER

If your friends are any fun at all, they are bound to get out of control at parties. This can be fun to a certain extent. Until their antics start to distract everyone from what they really should be paying attention to: YOU. When a guest starts to overshadow you, simply hide them in your guest bedroom until they've calmed down and/or passed out from drinking too much. Worried you won't be able to convince them to go lay down? A surefire trick for getting people to hide in your guest bedroom is by whispering into their ear, "Hey, I have to tell you a secret about Kendra. Come with me!" Then you guide them into the bedroom and as soon as they realize they're in a bedroom they'll hear the door slam, the click of the lock, and you cackling from outside the door while shrieking, "THAT'LL TEACH YOU TO UPSTAGE ME!"

So, now you know! Hosting a party is supereasy as long as you make sure to keep it simple and use as many mind manipulation tricks as possible! Now you try! Host a party this weekend!

yay

WHAT YOU NEED IN YOUR DUMB KITCHEN

WHITE DISHES

White dishes showcase the true look of your food better than dishes of a darker hue. This is because the white allows more light to bounce around the plate and shine through the food. Take a piece of lettuce, for example. On a black plate it's going to look darker and less appetizing because it has a certain amount of transparency to it. On a lighter plate, more light passes through it and makes it look appetizing and delicious. This is true of many foods, which is why most food looks better on a simple white palette. Keeping your dishware in a monochromatic white scheme also helps make sure everything works well together. If you have a fancy mansion with its own dish-storage wing, then by all means, go crazy collecting dishes in every color of the rainbow. But if you're just a regular person with limited dish storage, stick to an all-white dish scheme.

OIL, VINEGAR, SALT, PEPPER

It's my firm belief that if you're just getting started in the kitchen or just moving out on your own, the first four things you need are: olive oil, balsamic vinegar, sea salt, and a pepper mill for fresh ground pepper. You can make most simple recipes with these four things. Chicken? CHECK! Just add olive oil, salt, and pepper. Salad dressing? Combine olive oil and balsamic. Forgot butter? Put out a small container of olive oil with salt and pepper sprinkled over it for a magic dipping sauce. As with many things in life, simple is usually better than complicated.

CANISTERS TO HIDE YOUR SHAME

I try to keep the amount of kitchen countertop accessorizing to a minimum. The things that actually make the cut have to be pretty and fun to look at. This is why I like to store all my coffee, sugar, and other coffee-making paraphernalia in vintage inspired canisters (previous spread). This way, I don't have to worry about hiding them in the cupboard but also don't have to look at ugly bags of coffee, tea, and sugar. It also reminds me of the good old days before I was born, oldentimez when people used to buy things in bulk and keep them in cute containers in their homes. Before giant corporations overtook the food industry and started genetically engineering food to make us all obese.

A PLACE FOR YOUR SPICE COLLECTION TO GROW OVER TIME

When I moved into my first post-university apartment, I had zero dollars and very little in terms of kitchen supplies and other home goods. However, I had an interest in

cooking and would try out recipes whenever I could. The only problem was that every stupid recipe called for a spice I didn't have. Every time I would go shopping to make something, I'd end up spending a million dollars because I'd have to buy all these goddamn spices. So I started buying one random spice every time I shopped to build up my spice portfolio. AND SO CAN YOU! Purchasing a cute spice rack or defining another space to store all your cooking/baking items is a great way to keep them all organized and easily accessible so you don't accidentally buy them over and over again.

INTOXICATING VESSELS

I have a fetish for any kitchen accessory related to hosting. I think this is because in my fantasy life, I am just constantly throwing a dinner or cocktail party and it's always supereasy and I always have every single gadget I need for it. This is why I love having the correct drink servers for every imaginable occasion. Throwing a dinner party? You'll need a carafe for water. Throwing a birthday party? You'll need a large-scale cocktail dispenser. With the right drink dispensers, you'll ensure you and your loved ones are always at the optimum level of hydration and/or drunkenness.

HOW TO THROW A DINNER PARTY FOR LIKE NO MONEY

WHY HOST A DINNER PARTY?

One thing you realize when you get older is that you never really reach an age where you're like, "Cool. I'm a grown-up!" Instead, you just keep feeling like a kid forever and ever and ever and the only way you can feel even kind of like a grown-up is by mimicking stuff you've previously seen grown-ups doing. One of these things is having dinner parties. There seems to be no mature, more grown-up

thing to do on earth than to host or attend a dinner party. When I think of fancy, grown-up adults doing fancy grown-up things, the first thing I think of is dinner parties.

But why throw dinner parties? For me, they are a chance to catch up with friends without having to risk going out in public. A fun fact about me is that even just the thought of leaving the house forces me into an emotional tailspin that can only be soothed with a year's supply of horse tranquilizers or at least sixteen bottles of Whispering Angel Rosé. Here's a list of my issues with public spaces, most notably restaurants:

1. They're too loud
2. There's too many people in them
3. Not knowing how many people touched this table before I got here and if that rag that was used to wipe it off is filled with toxic mold spores
4. Questionable restaurant decor
5. When the waiter is listing the specials and you can tell he hates his life and wants to die and really just wishes you'd get out of his face
6. People who laugh too loud
7. People who don't understand how to talk without screaming directly into your ears
8. Uncooked red onions in sandwiches and salads
9. When the waiter comes to ask you how you like the food and it's always timed exactly after you've taken the biggest fucking bite of food you've ever taken in your whole life
10. Too hot/cold soup
11. Edison bulbs

Why is it that when other people are being superloud it's annoying but when you and your friends are being superloud it's way fun? Like it doesn't bother me when my friends are screaming their heads off but as soon as someone from another group starts yelling I'm like, "HOW DARE THEY!?!" Is it because as humans we secretly hate it when other people have fun that doesn't involve us? I've seriously always wondered this. Like I hate it when people are too loud (this isn't an old-person thing, I've always hated loud people at restaurants). But if it's a friend I'm like, "whatever that's fine."

So yeah, as I've outlined above, you should never go to a restaurant ever again. Especially to catch up with friends. If your goal is to deafen your ears with a cacophony of people screaming their terrible stories directly into your ears while you eat unhealthy food that always arrives at

an awkward time, then by all means go to a restaurant. But if you want to have a meaningful life in which you communicate with your friends and enjoy their company, I'd recommend throwing a dinner party.

ONE MYTH I NEED TO CLEAR UP BEFORE WE CAN MOVE ON

Before we can continue chatting about dinner parties, I need to clear up one myth about them. I always thought that cooking at home was a great way to save money. As someone who has been basically penniless since college, I always thought I was doing the responsible thing by asking people over to dinner instead of asking them out to dinner (this is for friends, not dates, that's a whole different story). Basically, if you look at cooking at home on a per-person basis, it is WAY cheaper than going out and seems like a good financial decision. But when I have people over I tend to just buy everything for everyone and guests will typically bring wine (sidenote: unless you are having huge financial difficulties, bring wine or something fun to share when you are invited to someone's home. NEVER SHOW UP EMPTY-HANDED. I feel that this is something that I shouldn't have to say, like everyone should know it, but it's something some people don't know. If you're sober or don't feel like drinking, a fun drink like sparkling lemonade or even plain old sparkling water will suffice. ANYTHING TO GUARD YOUR ARMS FROM EMPTINESS). So normally having a dinner party ends up being costlier than just going out to dinner. If you are on a strict budget, you can always ask people to bring stuff and make it a potluck, which is a fun way to engage people and make sure no one is spending too much. A good trick is to be like, "I'll make the main you bring the salad!" Your friend will be overjoyed that you trust her enough to contribute to the meal, thus cementing the friendship you share as her favorite and making you her very best friend.

One time, a friend of mine invited a group of people over and cooked dinner for them. The next day they all got an invoice asking them to pay for the share of the meal they ate. All of these friends had hosted this dude a million times, and were completely shocked and horrified that he would think to do something so crass. This would be something I'd file under: DON'T DO THIS EVER. If you're worried about cash, which I totally get, either offer to meet up with your friend at a reasonable restaurant or ask everyone to bring a dish to share. People don't mind bringing stuff to share. It's fun and it encourages everyone to eat things they make themselves, which is better for us anyway!

WHAT YOU'LL NEED

DISHES

You can buy the cheapest garbage food on earth and it'll look like a million bucks if it's plated nicely. As I've expressed elsewhere in this book (refer back to What You Need in Your Dumb Kitchen to see this rant), white dishes are my go-to. Having elegant place settings that match each other shows your guests you have your shit together.

PLATTERS–APLENTY!

I love a serving platter, so I love collecting them in piles so high that someday they will collapse on top of me, killing me instantly. You never know what you're going to need a serving platter for; making sure you stock up on them is a way to ensure your dinner parties are always stylish. I love simple wooden planks for serving cheese and vegetables, porcelain platters for serving fish and meats (hopefully not at the same time), and marble/stone trays for serving side dishes and appetizers.

BUY ONCE, USE A MILLION TIMES

To me, it doesn't feel like a real dinner if you're using paper plates and napkins. I think part of this comes from how I was raised (we never used disposable things like paper towels or paper plates). Dining with linen napkins, on real plates, using real glassware is a completely different experience than using paper plates, plastic cups, and disposable cutlery. You can be serving the most delicious food, but if it's on a paper plate the elegance is immediately lost. You can get very affordable cloth napkins and table linens at many a big box store. I'm not going to name them here because they didn't pay me any money to do so, but they rhyme with Blarget and Dykia.

THE SIMPLER THE BETTER

Something I've learned over the years is that simple is usually best. I tend to want to overcomplicate things, which often leads me to make way too much food that is way too complicated. My go-to meal to make for guests is simple, hearty, and healthy. It consists of the following:

MENU

Roasted Chicken with Carrots and Celery

Simple Side Salad

Cauliflower Rice

A simple, stunning country baguette

A fuck-ton of cheap-ass wine

DINNER IS READY, BUT IS YOUR TABLE???

The final aspect of hosting a dinner party, and the one that most typically sends me into a nearly psychotic state, is setting the table before people show up. I don't get fancy with dinner party table settings. But I do have a few tips for creating an inviting table scape:

1. LAYERING IS GOOD. Remember how in the '90s everyone in Seattle wanted to wear like seventeen layers so they'd look grunge and hip? Well, think of your dining table like it's a disgusting grungy Seattle hipster from the '90s and give him lots of layers. I like to layer place mats over tablecloths but that's a bit much for a weekday dinner party. So just make sure you have place mats and pretty white dishes laid over them before people arrive so they won't think you're a monster.

2. BUY SOME CHEAP-ASS FLOWERS. I like to grab flowers from my favorite bargain market. I'm not going to tell you what it's called because they aren't paying me (I'm still holding out), but I'll just say this place rhymes with Trader Ho's. Adding flowers, no matter how little you paid for them, will impress your guests and tell them the one thing you need them to know: that you come from money. Like old money, not new money like their trashy family.

3. WHEN DINNERTIME COMES, ASK THE FLOWERS TO STEP ASIDE. When guests arrive, it's nice to have flowers at the center of the table, but before everyone sits down, it's important to move them to the side so they don't obstruct anyone's view while you're all yelling as loud as you can trying to sound smarter than each other.

THE NIGHT IS OVER, AND SO IS YOUR LIFE

When dinner is over, you'll notice that you made about eight hundred dirty dishes and that your kitchen looks like a leprechaun covered in spaghetti tap-danced his way over every single surface (including the ceiling). Don't let the terror of seeing this mess distract you from hosting. If you start cleaning, your guests will leave. And then you'll be left alone to freak out about how awful everything in your life is and how truly lonely you feel all the time. I like to just leave dishes until the next morning, when I can listen to the radio, drink some coffee, and reflect on how great I am at throwing dinner parties.

BEGRUDGINGLY HOSTING A GUEST

Don't let them. Before they arrive, go into your refrigerator and check out what's inside. Ask yourself a few questions:

1. Does it look like a haunted beggar woman lives inside your refrigerator?

2. Will you ever eat those pickles in that moldy jar?

3. What brand is your ketchup? Is it store brand? If so, toss (unless it's Whole Foods, which is the only acceptable store brand because it makes it seem like you shop at a fancy store even though in real life no one REALLY shops there).

4. What is the color palette of your refrigerator? Does it say, "Happy Spring Day" or "Witch's Funeral?"

5. What story is the food in your refrigerator telling? Is it saying, "Hey, a happy person lives here who wakes up and goes jogging every morning and then comes home to cook organic breakfast for her whole family." Or does it say, "A desperate, lonely person lives here and every night when she comes home from work she eats tuna straight from the can while crying into a bowl of Diet Pepsi"? (She's using a bowl because all her glasses are dirty.)

SHOW YOUR GUEST HOW TO GET HIS OWN FUCKING WATER

One of my pet peeves is people being all, "Can I have a glass of water?" while I'm sitting, minding my own business, JUST TRYING TO LIVE MY FUCKING LIFE. Like, have these people never gotten their own glass of water? One time, I was at an extremely rich client's house. Like more servants than anyone whose home I've ever been in. And I've been in Gwyneth Paltrow's house. I'm pretty sure this rich client has never gotten her own glass of water. She just walks in the door and one of her attendants gets it for her. AND BRINGS IT TO HER IN A WINEGLASS ON A NAPKIN. Can

CLEAN ALL THE EMBARRASSING THINGS OUT OF YOUR REFRIGERATOR

Unwanted guests are usually terrible people with ugly souls who just want to come into your home and judge you.

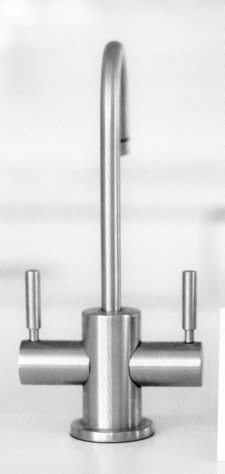

PURIFIED WATER

REUSABLE DRINKING BOTTLES

 YOU

you imagine going through that nonsense every time your mouth is dry? I'd kill myself. I hate interacting with staff. Mostly because I don't have any. The moral of the story is that getting glasses of water for people is fuckery and you should avoid it, like, always. Especially when the glass of water is for an unwanted guest.

To make sure no one asks you for a glass of water, ever, you can explain your water situation to them verbally or write them a little note. There are a ton of different ways people are drinking water today. Those big office-y jugs of water, tap water from the sink, individual bottles of water (major no-no but some people, who apparently have never heard of global warming and plastic-cancer, still do this), integrated water filtration systems. I have one of these filters installed, so I always show my guests how it works or if I'm not home I leave them a note about it. The subtext here is please don't ask me to get you a glass of water. This is not a restaurant and I am not your waiter.

LEAVE AN EXTRA TOOTHBRUSH FOR YOUR GUEST SO HE DOESN'T SECRETLY USE YOURS

My father is a dentist, so I have a thing for dental hygiene. Oftentimes, needy, unthoughtful guests will forget their toothbrushes and allow their filthy mouths to become even

more vile by the day. Finally, they will notice how disgusting they are, sneak into your bathroom, and brush their dirty little mouths with your pristine toothbrush. This is why it's a good idea to keep a supply of extra toothbrushes and toothpaste in your house in case someone disgusting shows up and needs to brush their teeth. You'll be doing everyone a favor by making sure they have what they need.

LEAVE THEM CHAMPAGNE TO GUILT THEM INTO BUYING YOU A HOST GIFT

Unwanted guests sometimes redeem themselves and become wanted guests by the end of their stay. This can be done in a number ways, but the easiest is by buying a host gift. Good examples of host gifts include a new car or a subscription to the L.A. Opera. There's also this leather jacket at Rag & Bone I've been looking at for a really long time but never have enough dollars to buy. Leaving champagne for your unwanted guest tells them, "This is a house where presents are given. GIVE ME SOMETHING."

LEAVE THEM A SNACK SO THEY WON'T BE HANGRY

The only thing worse than a despicable, selfish, needy unwanted guest is a despicable, selfish, needy, unwanted guest who's hungry. Your own hunger is a terrible affliction, a horrible feeling, an affront that must be dealt with. Trust me, I turn into a Gila monster when I get even the slightest bit hungry. But other people's hunger is just annoying and inconvenient and should be avoided at all costs. It's a scientific fact that being hungry makes people act like assholes. Do yourself a favor and leave a little snack out for your stupid guest so he or she won't get on your last nerve.

LEAVE YOUR GUEST A NOTE!

If you are out when your guest arrives, make sure to leave a note so he or she knows what to do and how to respond to being in your home. Tell him or her how you really feel. The note can say something like this:

Dear Unwanted Guest,

At first when I heard you were coming I was like, "YAY! Someone still loves me!" But then I remembered that one time when you were supposed to pick me up at the airport but instead went on a date with my ex-boyfriend and I had to take a cab and it was like $300 because of traffic and I didn't have cash and the cab driver wouldn't take a card for some weird reason so I ended up having to drive him to my bank but then I was mugged at the ATM and lost two of my limbs (I won't say which). Anyway, you're awful, WHAT ARE YOU DOING HERE? This is how you make me feel:

I wouldn't mind if you never came back.

Love,
Orlando

LEAVE OUT A CANDLE TO MASK YOUR GUEST'S DISGUSTING HUMAN SCENT

Another problem with guests is that they often leave your guest room smelling like human. If you have ever walked into a room right after someone has been sitting alone in there, breathing heavily and sweating profusely, you know what I'm talking about. One of my favorite ways to combat this odor is to leave a fresh scented candle for my guest. This does double duty, on one hand saying to your guest, "Hey, I'm thinking of you," while at the same time masking their disgusting smell.

FLAUNT FRESH-CUT FLOWERS

Nothing screams, "I AM PERFECT" at a guest like fresh-cut flowers. They're a great way to add freshness to a room as your guest's welcome grows stale.

AVOID GUESTS WHEN POSS

When I was little, there were twin beds in my room so oftentimes, when my family had a guest, they slept in the bed next to mine and told me scary ghost stories. I hated ghost stories, and thus I hated my guests. Long after they'd fallen asleep, I'd be laying there, FREAKING OUT about the ghosts they mentioned. Guests are dicks. They can be so invasive, time consuming, and selfish. And their ghost stories can be terrifying and childhood-ruining. What I learned from this experience is that you should just avoid having guests altogether, opting instead for alone time with your pets and/or a book you hold in your hands and pretend to read even though you're really just looking at your phone.

REMIND YOUR GUEST OF YOUR OPEN-DOOR POLICY

Reminding your unwanted guest that your door is always open to them not only reminds them they are welcome to come visit at any time, it also lets them know the door is open in case they'd like to use it to leave your house and never come back.

MAKE THE GUEST ROOM WARM, INVITING, AND PLAYFUL

Guest rooms are a chance to use furniture and decor you might not put in a space that gets used every day. You can be a little more adventurous in there because if the design ends up being too busy or loud, you don't have to look at it every day. For example, I added a superfun gallery wall to my guest bedroom and it makes the whole space feel like a lively, art-filled retreat. I normally wouldn't be a proponent of having gallery walls in bedrooms (HOW U SUPPOSED TO SLEEP WITH ALL THAT CHAOS?) but since it's a guest room, it totally works. Think of guest rooms as a great test dummy for ideas you'd like to try elsewhere in your house.

HOW TO BE YOUR OWN MAID

Everyone agrees, cleaning sucks. It's boring, you have to do it over and over, and it's never really done. When I was little and I had to clean my room, I used to throw everything into my closet then put a beach towel over it and hope no one noticed. I never got away with it, which is probably why I turned into such a zealot about cleanliness. You see, cleaning sucks, but having a clean house is the one thing that separates us from the animals (well, that and coffee tables, but we'll get to that later). If we allow ourselves to live in filthy caves like lions, we'll be just as wild and crazy as they are. And if we allow our homes to fall into such disarray, soon our place at the top of the food chain will be compromised and a talking bear will become president. IS THAT WHAT YOU WANT?

DON'T CALL THEM "MAIDS"

While this section is about how to clean your own house, I recognize that some of the rich and famous people reading this probably have housekeepers. Which brings me to one of my grievances. Don't call your housekeeper a "maid." To me, that's always seemed gauche. Like, this is not nineteenth-century England, and you are not an aristocratic heiress living in a storied estate with your parents when suddenly a mysterious stranger, Mister Lovingslyshiregateshire, comes to live with your family and causes an unexpected folly between you and your sisters.

I don't know why it bothers me so much, but I have found over the years that the type of people who usually use the word "maid" are the type of people who are really ostentatious and tacky. There is something very crass and classless about the term. It's like calling someone a "servant" (that's literally part of the definition of "maid," look it up!). Anyway, don't be gross. Maybe it's because I grew up in California, where we tend to use the word "housekeeper," "maid" just rubs me the wrong way.

So yeah, if you are lucky enough to have someone helping you clean your house, give them the respect they deserve and call them a housekeeper. Or a cleaner. Or a cleaning lady. Or a cleaning gentleman. ANYTHING BUT MAID OK!?!

GET A GODDAMN FUNCTIONING VACUUM CLEANER

Terrible ineffectual vacuum cleaners are my number-one pet peeve of all time (next to cherry tomatoes and uncooked onions in my salad). Why? Because a vacuum that works is such a joy. It's like the most efficient form of cleaning. Unlike sweeping or dusting, which just basically launches potentially infectious particles directly into your mouth and nose, vacuuming sucks it all up into a handy machine and gets it out of your life forever. The downside: MOST PEOPLE HAVE GARBAGE VACUUMS!

Why? Because the vacuum industry is now dominated by cheap, throwaway vacuum cleaners made of plastic, designed to work for nine months then break down, forcing you to have to buy a new vacuum, throw away the current one, and slowly fill up landfills with these trash vacuums. This annoys me firstly because it's terrible for the planet, secondly because it provides an inferior vacuuming experience.

My advice? Spend time researching a high-quality vacuum that can be repaired if it breaks. Spending a lot more money up front might be scary, but think about it over the course of ten to fifteen years. If you're buying a new vacuum every year that's a huge expense to both you and the planet. SAVE THE PLANET YOU'RE OUR ONLY HOPE, otherwise we're gonna all be skeletons melting in the sun in like three years.

USE REUSABLE CLEANING CLOTHS

Everything I use to clean is reusable. I have a reusable floor mop system and reusable cloths for the rest of the cleaning tasks. This is not only because this is better for the environment, this is also because actual cloth cleans way better than paper towels. You have to use like three hundred paper towels to do the job of two reusable cleaning cloths. You end up wasting a lot of money on disposable floor cleaning pads and other disposable products AND THEY ARE INFERIOR TO THE REUSABLE KINDS THAT HAVE BEEN AROUND FOREVER. Save yourself and our Mother (Earth) by investing in some quality reusable cleaning products.

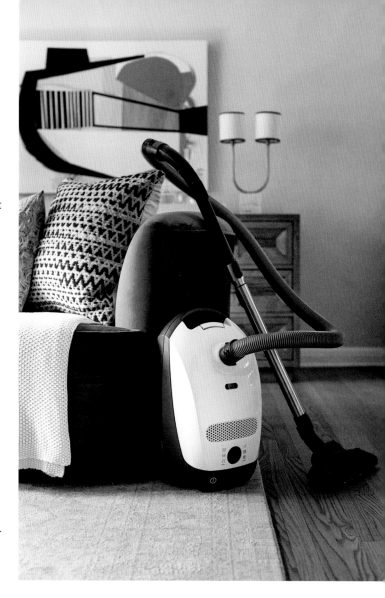

REGULARLY ROTATE TABLE LINENS AND OTHER TABLETOP ACCESSORIES

Even if you're not using them, tabletop accessories get dusty after about a week. If you've set the dinner table and haven't sat down to a meal in weeks, swap it out. If you have a coffee table full of cute accessories, take them all off every week or two and wipe them down. The added bonus here is that this constantly keeps your surface styling fresh and tight.

NOT SURE HOW TO THROW A THROW?

Perfectly throwing a throw is a very difficult, specific art form. If you're not sure how your skills match up, you can make sure your throw looks neat and tidy by folding it in thirds or quarters and hanging over the end of a sofa or large-scale chair. This serves as a reminder to you and your guests that you are not a barbarian and that you take care of your things.

CLEAN AS YOU GO

The only thing worse than cleaning is cleaning after you've let your place go for weeks and weeks and weeks. If you stay on top of your tasks by taking 5–10 minutes every morning to straighten up, you save yourself the boring agony of having to do a megaclean after you've let your house turn into a pigsty. If you feel too busy to do this, make a note of how long it actually takes you to do this daily mini-clean. It'll be a lot less time than you think it is (the mind makes it seem longer because, let's face it, you hate cleaning and are no better than the animals).

PLANT YOUR RAGE IN A CONTAINER GARDEN

WHERE DID YOUR RAGE COME FROM?

Have you ever been trapped walking behind a group of tourists in New York City, waddling slowly, shoulder to shoulder, while you're trying to get to work and it's 95 degrees with 4,000 percent humidity and you're an hour late for work because your train was delayed? Have you ever ordered a salad and asked for ABSOLUTELY NO ONIONS and then the salad arrives, smothered in uncooked red onions and then you have to pick them out and then your hands smell like disgusting red onions for the next two days and you're literally on the verge of barfing? Have you ever taken a date to a friend's function only to have him fall in love with your friend and immediately get married like literally at the same party even though you two are still technically on a date? If any of the above has happened to you, it's likely you'll respond with something called RAGE.

Rage can take many forms. Maybe you find yourself waking up, sitting at a 90-degree angle, and yelling at the ceiling every morning because WHY IS LIFE SO HARD. Maybe you spend hours a day maniacally lecturing your refrigerator about how it's her fault you've gained weight ("MAYBE YOU SHOULDN'T BE FILLED WITH SUCH DELICIOUS FOOD, FRIDGE!"). Maybe you involuntarily get resting bitch face every time someone says, "Oh, your name is Orlando? ARE YOU FROM FLORIDA?!?" and then laughs for twenty minutes at their dumb joke. The point is, everyone experiences rage. It's a normal, healthy part of being a person with a brain and eyeballs. Or without eyeballs. Rage doesn't discriminate.

For me, rage comes most intensely when I'm in the TSA line at the airport. It normally goes like this:

TSA: TAKE YOUR SHOES OFF AND PUT YOU LAPTOP IN THE BIN.

ME: OK.

TSA: WHY ARE YOUR SHOES OFF? WE TOLD YOU NOT TO TAKE THEM OFF!

ME: OK.

TSA: SIR! SIR! SIR! SIR! SIR! SIR! SIR! SIR! SIR! SIR! SIR! SIR! SIR! SIR! SIR! SIR! SIR! SIR! SIR! SIR! SIR! SIR! SIR! SIR! SIR! SIR! SIR! SIR! SIR! SIR! SIR! SIR! SIR! SIR! SIR! SIR! SIR! SIR! SIR! . . . We told you to leave your laptop in the case. WHY DID YOU TAKE IT OUT???

ME: But you di—

TSA: SIR! MA'AM? IT? PLEASE KEEP THE LINE MOVING.

ME: [*Moves through line.*]

TSA: WAIT YOUR TURN SIR YOU CAN'T CUT IN LINE LIKE THAT. SIR! SIR! SIR! SIR! SIR! SIR! SIR! SIR! SIR! SIR! SIR! SIR! SIR! SIR! SIR! SIR! SIR! SIR! SIR! SIR! SIR!

(Sidenote: screaming "sir," "ma'am," or "CALM DOWN" is a surefire way to fill anyone with rage.)

TSA: HURRY UP PLEASE PUT YOUR SHOES ON SOMEWHERE ELSE.

ME: OK.

TSA: WHAT ARE YOU DOING YOU CAN'T PUT YOUR SHOES ON THERE!

OK, so I'm basically just using this chapter to complain about the TSA. But I think I have a good point. I mean, one time I was in a mass shooting at LAX and the TSA literally did nothing. They just ran away from the shooter,

STEPS TO COMPOSING YOUR SUCCULENT GARDEN

1. With each succulent still in its plastic container, figure out what your composition is going to be. You can do this by sticking them inside whatever pot they're going in and looking at them with an intense glare until you're absolutely positive that you like the way you've arranged them. Remember, there is no going back after you've placed the succulents into the soil. If you get this wrong, the whole rest of your life could be negatively affected. Which maybe isn't so bad, to be honest, maybe it'll just add to your already healthy amount of rage.

2. Haphazardly pour a bunch of soil into your pot. Pretend you're pouring it onto the face of that terrible waiter who was like, "Yah yah I get it, no onions," and then put tons of uncooked red onions on your salad. WHY WOULD ANYONE EVER PUT RAW ONIONS ON A SALAD? COOKED ONIONS ARE DELICIOUS. RAW ONES ARE NASTY.

3. Shove all the succulents into the dirt. The same way people have been pushing you down your ENTIRE LIFE.

4. Clean up the huge mess you've made by watering the succulents VERY LIGHTLY with a watering can or hose. Speaking of hose, YOUR MOM.

like pushing their way over us to get out. I guess my point is that you should be terrified when you're at the airport. And you have every reason to be filled with rage at the TSA people. They're just yelling at you to yell at you because yelling at people feels good. And it's natural for you to respond with rage, because it's a totally normal response to having people who really can't do anything to protect you yell at you over and over again. NOT THAT I'M SCARRED FROM THAT SHOOTING OR ANYTHING.

WHY HOLD ON TO RAGE?

1. It keeps life from getting too boring.
2. It keeps you energized.
3. Like caffeine, it helps cleanse pores and keeps skin looking fresh and young.
4. You can use it against the people you hate.
5. It increases your heart rate and thus increases your metabolism, making you skinny!
6. It's medically impossible to get rid of.

WILL GARDENING HELP?

Probably not, but it's nice to try. Life will likely keep throwing things your way that will continue to outrage you. Gardening will likely not calm your rage, but it will give you a place to manifest it physically. That way, every time you look at a plant you can be like, "My rage is in there!"

COMPOSING THE PERFECT SUCCULENT CONTAINER GARDEN

When composing a succulent arrangement, you should buy succulents in a variety of heights, colors, and textures. You'll want at least one tall one, a few medium-sized ones, and a lot of smaller, filler succulents to fill the holes.

YOUR PLANTS ARE GONNA DIE

Now is as good a time as any to tell you something very important about the indoor succulent arrangement I just encouraged you to create: IT'S 100 PERCENT FOR SURE GOING TO DIE. Succulents don't like living inside. So even if you put it by a window, it's going to die. Before you get all pissy and start freaking out at me for making you do this, remember, rage is best directed inward. But also, think about it. Do you ever buy flowers? Flowers are already dead when you buy them. But succulents will live happily inside for 3–5 months before quickly dying and leaving you alone to wallow in your pain.

If you're smart, you'll get rid of the succulents before they get old and gross. This is what all my ex-boyfriends did with me. Instead of waiting for something you're not interested in to age so much, why not just get a new one you like even better! Everyone wins! Well, everyone else wins. YAY?

WHAT TO DO WHEN YOU KILL YOUR PLANT, WHICH IS INEVITABLE SO DON'T EVEN TRY NOT TO KILL IT

If your plants start to look sad, it's a good idea to replant them outside like the main characters in pseudofeminist empowerment stories like *Eat Pray Love* or *Under the Tuscan Sun*, a refreshing moment outdoors will do wonders for the souls of your dying succulents. Like Gay Men in Palm Springs or Woo Girls* in cut-up Coachella shorts, succulents love hot, sunny, arid situations. They will revive after a few days of sun, fun, and heat.

*A WOO GIRL IS A GIRL WHOSE MAIN VOCABULARY CONSISTS OF INTERMITTENT VARIATIONS ON THE WORD "WOO!" WOOING NORMALLY HAPPENS UPON ENTERING A ROOM AND/OR SOCIAL SITUATION, BUT CAN REALLY BE DONE AT ANY TIME. NOTHING GETS BETWEEN A WOO GIRL AND HER "WOO."

WHEN YOUR SUCCULENTS GET ALL STRUNG OUT AND NASTY LIKE STREETWALKING DRUG ADDICTS

There comes a time in all of our lives where we are strung out and crazy, like drug addicts at the end of our rope. Mine is probably right now, to be honest, but it comes at a different time for everyone. It's the same with plants. Succulents start out cute and smooth and perky. But over time, they tend to get leggy and weird-looking. And that's when it's time to cut them down and start over again. The great thing about succulents is that they're incredibly resilient and can survive anything. So when they start to get leggy, I like to chop them up and force them to grow the way I want them to grow. If life has taught me one thing, it's that you should definitely try to force everything around you to look and grow exactly how you want it to.

HOW TO REFRESH YOUR NASTY-ASS OVERGROWN SUCCULENT

1. First, remove any dried brown leaves or overgrowth around the base of each succulent.

2. Then, locate the offshoots that have gotten too long/leggy.

3. CHOP THOSE OFFSHOOTS TO THE BASE OF THEIR STEMS.

4. Clean any dead leaves from those offshoots and set aside.

5. Create holes using a chopstick (preferably the disposable kind you get from takeout).

6. Insert the trimmed-down offshoots into the holes.

7. Water and set aside.

That's it! Succulents literally survive this. Like they really don't even need their roots. It's a goddamn Christmas miracle.

And there you go, YOU DID IT! You contained your rage in a container garden. Or at least you gave yourself some time to think about your rage while gardening. And what fun is rage if you can't spend hours of your day pondering it, right?

LIFE ADVICE

You guys, guess what? You're in luck! As fate would have it, my life turned into a raging Dumpster fire while I was writing this book. I know that doesn't sound very lucky but it means I have all sorts of fun insights to share with you about what to do when your life turns upside down. Just got laid off? NO PROBLEM! Boyfriend dumped you? WHO CARES! This chapter is all about how to roll with life's punches, or at least how to complain about them until you feel adequately satisfied. This chapter will thrill and delight you, or at the very least make you thankful you aren't me.

LIVING WITH A ROOMMATE OR BOYFRIEND IS TERRIBLE

HUMANS ARE INNATELY AWFUL AND SHOULD REALLY JUST LIVE ALONE IN CAVES

One basic fact about humanity is that in our innermost hearts, we all just want to murder each other. We are all animals pretending not to be animals. And this becomes blatantly obvious when we try to cohabitate with a friend or loved one. A woman who seems sweet and amazing when you meet will turn out to be a totally disgusting pig the second you decide to be roommates. A guy you think is whimsical and artistic turns out to be a complete fucking psychopath the second you fall in love and move in together.

It's a medical fact that human beings probably shouldn't live together. We should live in caves—ALONE—left to our own devices to protect ourselves against the bears and mountain lions that want to bite our heads off and eat our bodies like sashimi. But for some dumb reason, we've created a society based on the idea that people will live with their partners, or worse, live with random people from the Internet. This is bound to create a variety of unbearable results. Most notably having to put up with someone else's bullshit on a daily basis. Having them stand in your way while you're trying to brush your teeth. Having them forget to style the bedside tables EXACTLY how you want them. The list of offenses is endless.

I've perfected living with roommates and boyfriends over the years. The main thing I've learned in my extensive experience is to do the opposite of whatever you want to do. For example, if your boyfriend leaves a bunch of dirty dishes in the sink over the weekend while you're away so that when you come home your whole apartment smells like toxic mold, your first instinct will be to find a sword and cut his body in half. DO NOT DO THIS. Instead, be like, "Honey, good to see you! I'm gonna do these dishes!" Later, while he sleeps, create a voodoo doll that bears a striking resemblance to him. Stab it with a sharp kitchen knife repeatedly. Then throw it away and pretend nothing happened. You'll feel better and no one will have to know that you got all your aggression out on a tiny doll!

Below I outline a few more tips for how to live with a roommate without losing your mind!

HIRE A HOUSEKEEPER

Most fights that happen between roommates occur because one roommate is sloppy and disgusting and the other roommate is neat and perfect. I'm usually the neat, perfect one and my roommate is usually the gross, disgusting one. I had one particularly gross roommate when I first moved to New York who used to get mad at me if I touched any of his belongings. I learned my lesson quickly after cleaning up after him one too many times and having him freak out about it. He had a goldfish and I used to clean its bowl because he never changed the water but then he started getting mad at me about that so I stopped. AND THE GOLDFISH DIED YOU GUYS. Like literally because his bowl was so dirty. I've lived with the weight of that death on my shoulders for years. LET THIS BE A LESSON TO ALL OF US NOT TO BE DISGUSTING OR YOUR FISH WILL DIE AND IT WILL BE ALL YOUR FAULT. Let this also be a lesson that if you're ever going to get along with your roommate, you're going to need a housekeeper. Can't afford a housekeeper? Move somewhere cheaper and get a housekeeper. THE HOUSEKEEPER IS LITERALLY THE

ONLY THING THAT WILL KEEP YOU FROM MURDERING YOUR ROOMMATE IN HIS SLEEP FOR BEING SUCH A DISGUSTING PIG.

DON'T LET YOUR ROOMMATE CATCH YOU READING HIS DIARY

Listen, we all know you're going to snoop in your roommate's stuff and invade his privacy. That's totally normal as a roommate. Who doesn't dig through her roommate's underwear drawer or read her roommate's texts while he's in the bathroom? Totally normal roommate behavior. But etiquette teaches us you have to be sneaky enough about this stuff that you don't get caught. Look how pissed I got when my roommate read my diary!

ESTABLISH GROUND RULES FOR BASIC HUMAN DECENCY

As humans, we're all vile, disgusting beings with base needs, desires, and horrible revolting habits. However, when you live with a partner it's important to pretend to be as non-disgusting as possible. Thus, if your partner does something gross, it's important to tell him as soon as possible in the gentlest way you can. For example, if he thinks it's OK to chow down on pizza while in bed, SLAP THAT PIZZA OUT OF HIS HAND and be like, "THINK ABOUT MY LINEN SHEETS BABE!" He'll understand his folly and never do it again. And you'll have the satisfaction of knowing that when he dumps you and starts dating someone else you will have left him a better man than he was to begin with.

DON'T TEXT AT DINNER

According to scientists everywhere, the number-one reason for divorce is texting at the dinner table. I don't have a boyfriend because mine dumped me while I was writing this book, so I had to trick my friend Jeffery Self into playing one for this photo. But if I did have one I would be pissed if he was staring at his phone the whole time I was trying to give him loving googly eyes. Appropriate dinner table behaviors include hand-petting, prolonged eye contact, intense philosophical discussion, fighting about inane differences of opinion, and talking shit about mutual friends. Duh.

WHAT TO DO WHEN ALL YOUR FRIENDS HAVE BABIES AT ONCE

I'M A DESIGNER, WHY IS THIS HAPPENING TO ME?

There comes a time in every designer's life when he has to confront the one must-have accessory missing from his life: a baby. It's not that he even wanted a baby in the first place, it's just that everyone else has one or is in the process of making/buying one. This can be a traumatic experience for a designer because we're used to getting everything we want, even if it means we have to steal it from the people we love most. Designers are ruthless and cannot be satisfied. This is why we get particularly outraged when people beat us out at certain life events. Like having babies. If life is a competition (it is), designers will always be in first place. And if we're not, we'll cheat our way until we get there.

In all honesty, it's pretty weird when all your friends start having kids. For me, it was around age thirty-three. I had one friend who had kids way early (at age twenty), but everyone else in my life was busy acting like a kid still, eating Apple Jacks and jumping on Mom and Dad's beds in a sleeping bag until age thirty. I think the real reason it can be jarring when friends have babies is that it makes you feel like they're moving onto the next part of life. Meanwhile, you're in stasis. Kind of waiting for another chapter of life to begin. BUT LIKE WHAT IF THAT CHAPTER NEVER BEGINS???

Life is filled with milestones until you graduate from college. Like going from grammar school to middle school. Middle school to high school. High school and college graduation. But then all of a sudden it stops. Like—BOOM—college graduation, no more fun milestones

until you get married. And if you don't get married, say, for example, because the only two serious boyfriends you've ever had had absolutely no interest in marrying you because you're gross (NOT THAT THIS EVER HAPPENED TO ME! YES IT HAS OK BYE), then you have even fewer milestones to add to your scrapbook.

Life feels like it makes sense until your thirties. There's like a logical progression from A to B to C. But then without warning it's like that Peggy Lee song "IS THAT ALL THERE IS" and you're like "WHAT NEXT?" For some people, the answer is easy. JUST PLOP OUT A BABY. For the rest of us, it's like, "WHAT DO WE DO ABOUT THAT BABY THAT JUST EXPLODED OUT OF MY FRIEND???"

Whenever anything unexpected or unfavorable happens to me, I have the same response. I usually look at whoever is next to me and scream, "I AM A DESIGNER! WHY IS THIS HAPPENING TO ME!" This gets their attention and lets them know that because I am a designer I am not only more important than they are, but I am also more sensitive and have more feelings. This way they know they should be superattentive to me and pay attention only to me, especially if there's a baby in the room. Child psychologists agree: there are long-lasting psychological damages associated with ignoring a designer in the presence of an infant. WE HAVE MANY NEEDS BUT OUR NEED FOR ATTENTION SURPASSES THEM ALL.

WHY BABIES?

Before you allow a baby to grow inside yourself or in the body of someone you love, think about whether the void you're trying to fill could be filled with something less time-consuming, loud, and inconvenient for your gay friends who just want to party with you. Are you being selfish? Couldn't you get the same stupid satisfaction by buying a new purse or a more expensive car? Let's be real, a baby's gonna cost way more than a fancy Mercedes in the long run. Choose the car, dude.

I have a trick for whenever I want to have a baby. I drive up to Ojai, look for a cute store, and buy myself a piece of pottery. Pottery is just as satisfying as a human child but with a lot less fuss and a lot less noise pollution (SERIOUSLY

WHY ARE BABIES YELLING ALL THE TIME!?!). So if your ovaries start to hurt every time you see a baby, run to your nearest artisanal boutique and buy some pottery. It'll quench your thirst for a baby and will give you ample accessories to style your bookcase, which is looking kinda sad quite honestly.

BABIES: THE WORST STD?

It's time you learned the cold, hard facts about infants:

1. Babies are incurable. Once you have one, you cannot get rid of it ever. So you better be into that baby when you have it, because it's never going away. Take it from me. I'm a thirty-five-year-old grown-up baby (who was once an infant myself!) who recently lived with his parents. Think about that when you decide on having a baby. What will you even be doing in thirty-five years?

2. According to scientists, babies are technically a parasite. They attach themselves to your body and suck out the nutrients you need. This leads to fatigue, and the creeping feeling that you are never truly able to have time to yourself, that if you run off to hide in a corner of the house your baby will home in on your location and come to terrorize you.

3. Babies are like an alarm system that can go off at any time. You know those car alarms that go off and keep going for hours and hours because the stupid person who owns the car is nowhere to be found? A baby is like that.

4. Babies think only about their own needs and have absolutely no interest or consideration for your feelings. They only care about what you can do for them and they'll stop at nothing to get their way 100 percent of the time.

5. Babies aren't supposed to look at TV/phone screens for at least two years. WHAT ARE YOU SUPPOSED TO DO FOR THOSE TWO YEARS? NOT LOOK AT SCREENS? This is stupid.

WHY WON'T THAT BABY BE QUIET AND LISTEN TO MY PROBLEMS?

If you encounter a baby, ask him calmly and firmly to please listen to every word you say and do exactly as you ask. If baby does not respond favorably to this, go and find his mother and give him back immediately. After all, you're not the one who decided to have this baby. You will die alone, screaming from your deathbed, "IF ONLY I'D HAD A BABY SO THERE WAS SOMEONE TO CHILL WITH ME RIGHT NOW THAT'S SERIOUSLY THE ONLY REASON I WOULD HAVE HAD A BABY BUT I NEVER GOT AROUND TO IT OK BYE WORLD!"

BRIBING BABY: GIFT BUYING TO MAKE BABY LIKE YOU MORE THAN EVERYONE ELSE

Babies love presents. Even if you hate a baby, you need to make sure that baby loves you more than she loves everyone else IN THE WORLD. The reason for this is that someday, during the apocalypse when you are quite old and feeble, you may need the baby (who at that point will be a virile, strong youth) to save you from alien invaders. It may be the kind of situation where Grown-Up Baby will have to choose to save just one person, letting everyone else be murdered by Alien Ghosts. So at that point it is very important that you be Grown-Up Baby's very favorite person on earth. Buying the right gifts for baby will ensure that she doesn't let the aliens get you.

Babies are pretty easy to buy for. Choose a gift for a baby based on texture and color. Don't worry about how appropriate it is. Say, for example, you give a baby a set of stabbing knives. You'll wrap the gift, let baby open it, and she'll immediately want to play with the knives. When Dad takes the knives away squealing, "WHAT KIND OF PSYCHOPATH GIVES KNIVES TO A BABY!?!" the baby will immediately burst into tears, recognizing that Dad took away the present she wanted to play with. This memory will imprint upon baby's brain. Years from now, as Ghost Alien Invaders are blasting Dad with a ray gun, Grown-Up

Baby will look him directly in the eyes and say, "I remember that time with the stabbing knives!" You'll be saved, your extensive gift buying will have paid off, and you and Grown-Up Baby will be BEST FRIENDS. ALSO: YOU'LL BE ALIVE!

WHAT TO DO WHEN BABY IS DRESSED BETTER THAN YOU

Nothing pisses me off more than when a baby is dressed better than me. So if you're a mom, think about me before putting your baby in an adorable outfit I'm going to be jealous of. When the baby that's in this photo shoot showed up in those overalls I immediately flew into a diva rage. WHY DOES HE GET THE CUTE OVERALLS AND I'M WEARING THIS GARBAGE OUTFIT? I calmed down after a while but my response was completely valid and any rational adult would have responded the same way. So keep this in mind next time you put your kid in an outfit that costs more than the one I'm wearing, K?

If we've learned anything in this chapter it's that when you're thinking about having a baby you should first think about me. And after you've determined whether your baby will have a net benefit to me (perhaps by saving me from murderous Alien Ghosts), then you should go ahead. Babies are the must-have accessory of the season, but are you really ready for your baby? AM I REALLY READY FOR YOUR BABY? Think of the consequences . . .

WHAT TO DO WHEN YOU GAIN 50 POUNDS

AM I FAT AND GROSS?

One of the first questions I remember asking myself upon seeing a mirror for the first time was "Am I fat and gross?" I don't know how a three-year-old would know to ask this question, but I did. I have always had a crazy complex about my body. And I'm not entirely sure where it comes from. One theory is that it comes from my mother's own paranoia about her own body. She was always on a diet. My father, on the other hand, was always thin because he had completely different genetics (not sure why I got zero of those genetics THANKS FOR NOTHING, SCIENCE).

The first time I remember being actively excited about losing weight was when I was seven. I got tonsillitis and I couldn't eat anything for days. Simultaneously, my sister's dance teacher had roped me into playing King Triton in a ballet version of *The Little Mermaid* (this was the '90s, after all). Weirdly, I had to be shirtless for this. When I couldn't eat for weeks because my tonsils were swollen and I lost tons of weight, I remember being really happy because I wouldn't look fat for this dumb dance recital. I WAS SEVEN FUCKING YEARS OLD. Have you seen a seven-year-old? They're essentially infants.

The first real diet I went on was when I was twelve (still technically an infant). I joined Weight Watchers with my mom and had to go to these weird meetings with lots of ladies dressed like *Sister Wives* and weigh in every week. It was quite a strange environment for a twelve-year-old boy. But I wanted to do it. I am thirty-five years old now and I cannot remember a time in my life when I wasn't obsessed by my weight and ashamed of my body.

I will always identify as a fat person. I think this is something a lot of FFKs (Former Fat Kids) do. Once you have been a fat person, you will always identify as one and

feel kinship with other fat people, regardless of what you look like on the outside. As I've gotten older (and more consistently thin for longer periods of time), I've had to come to terms with my own thin privilege. Thin privilege is exactly what it sounds like. If you can fit into an airline seat or buy clothing from a regular store, you have thin privilege. But having thin privilege doesn't stop us from CONSTANTLY FREAKING OUT ABOUT OUR BODIES.

I'm not sure who has it worse in terms of body image, women or gay men. Women can be extremely hard on themselves and each other when it comes to their bodies. But if you ask most gay men, they'll tell you there is little wiggle room in the gay community when it comes to bodies. You're allowed to have a perfect body or a really perfect body. BUT WHAT ABOUT BEARS, YOU ASK? (Bears are supposed to be fluffier, thicker, hairy guys.) Bears are basically regular (perfect and hot) gay guys just with hair. The gay community is basically one big pie of body oppression.

WHO CAN I BLAME FOR THIS?

Blaming is one of my favorite pastimes, so naturally I've always looked for someone to blame for having to choose between being fat and being on a constant diet. It's obvious to anyone who has struggled with their weight that genetics is the biggest contributor to why we're fat. For most of my life I blamed myself for how fat I was. But the first time I lived with a boyfriend who was genetically very thin, I realized that I'd been given the short end of the stick metabolically. He'd eat twice as much as me and be worried about losing weight while I would eat less, work out more, and still gain weight.

I'm not bringing this up to make you feel sorry for me (although please, feel free, I love pity). I'm bringing it up because nothing makes me more furious than people who have never been fat judging fat people. If you've never struggled with your weight you have no place making any judgments about why another person might be overweight. For some reason fat shaming is one of the last forms of discrimination that is still socially acceptable. I'm not gonna come in here and be PC police or anything, I just think it's uncool. People struggle with their weight for a variety of reasons, but if you've been skinny all your life you can just keep your theories as to why we're fat to yourself.

POSSIBLE SOLUTIONS

ACCEPTING YOURSELF AS YOU ARE: I know this sounds completely insane. But it turns out that instead of obsessing about your body it's possible that addressing the issues in your brain might have a better net positive effect on your life. I think a certain amount of self-discipline is helpful for staying healthy. But do you have self-discipline or an eating disorder? When it comes to issues of nutrition, you can't be too careful.

EXERCISING ALL THE TIME: This is fun if you have time and don't mess up your joints. Added bonus: ENDORPHINS!

DIETS: The more diets I've tried, the less I believe in them (though I am going to outline one fun one below). Basically, I think they just slow your metabolism and then you gain weight when you inevitably go off your diet because we're not robots and being on a diet sucks.

GIVING UP BOOZE: This totally works, but is so boring. You get more used to it after the first week. (Note: do not attempt if all your friends are boozehounds with loose morals.)

ORLANDIET

And now the moment you've all been waiting for, the moment I reveal the diet and exercise tricks that have kept me looking twenty at age sixty-seven. I invented my own diet and it's called Orlandiet. Basically, this diet was born when I was doing set design/art department work on movies and music videos. If you've never been on a real-life Hollywood set before, let me fill you in on a little secret: the food on Hollywood sets is garbage. I have no idea why, considering that everyone in the movies is supposed to be skinny, but the food on set is all candy and carbs. So I had to come up with a special diet to keep myself from exploding, and I'm going to share it with you now. It's pretty simple:

DON'T EAT ANYTHING WITH INGREDIENTS IN IT.

This may sound ridiculous, but it's actually pretty helpful. Especially on Hollywood sets. The premise of the diet is that you don't eat anything where you can't see each individual ingredient. For example, you can eat a grape (it's just one ingredient, grapes!) but you can't eat an M&M (it's a combination of a ton of ingredients you can't see with your eyes).

Here's a sample of things you can and cannot eat on this diet:

Do:
+ Salad (you can see all the ingredients since they are just chopped up vegetables)
+ Apples
+ Giant chunks of meat
+ Nuts
+ Dried fruit
+ Pretty much any vegetable
+ As much coffee as you can handle
+ Basically anything where you can see the ingredients with your naked eyes, except dairy

Don't:
+ Bread
+ Dairy
+ Cookies
+ Cheese (I don't know how cheese is made and I DON'T WANT TO KNOW so I'm gonna assume it has lots of ingredients)
+ Cake
+ Pizza
+ Hamburgers
+ Most delicious things
+ Nutrition bars
+ Booze
+ Basically anything where you can't see the individual ingredients with your bare eyes

Obviously, this Orlandiet is basically a rip-off of every trendy diet that has existed for the past twenty years. I'm not a nutritionist and I don't claim to have a scientific knowledge of how to take your body from TUBBY to TONED in ten minutes. What I can say is that the less processed and complicated your food is, the healthier you'll be. Steering clear of ingredients is one (very oversimplified) way of avoiding eating the wrong things. You kind of already know what you can and can't eat. The reason diet books help with that is they remind you of one simple fact: don't eat garbage processed food and you'll feel way better ALSO SORRY YOUR LIFE WILL BE BORING.

Writing the above made me wanna go to France and eat a baguette smothered in salty French butter. DIETS ARE BORING!

ULTIMATELY, IT HAS TO BE FOR YOU AND IT HAS TO BE FUN

Take it from someone who has been on a diet for twenty-three years, you're never going to get anywhere if you're doing it for someone else or for the wrong reasons. You have to approach diet/exercise/health from a fun perspective and take it on as a fun hobby or you're going to get bored with it or feel like it's punishment. Also, you have to start from a place of self-acceptance. That's the hardest part, to be honest. Truly being OK with your body and recognizing how lucky you are to inhabit it and be alive. The alternative, starting from a place of hating your body and wanting to change it, only leads to disappointment in the long run, because you'll never reach your ideal body fast enough to assuage your self-hate.

I look back at pictures of myself from when I was thinner than now and fatter than now and I have one common thought: I wish I hadn't hated my body so much at that point. The memory of how much time I've spent over the years worrying about my weight and what I looked like weighs on me. I regret all the time I've wasted feeling bad about myself. But I've never regretted any of the time I've spent feeling confident. The greatest gift you can give yourself is self-affirmation.

So yeah, by all means have fun doing stupid trendy diets and working out and being conscientious about your health. But also have the self-awareness to realize you're just a person doing your best and you are great the way you are. Don't seek outside affirmation. That will just lead to the desire for more outside affirmation. You have to find this esteem on your own, from inside yourself. THE CALL IS COMING FROM INSIDE THE HOUSE!

YOU ARE GORGEOUS END OF STORY BYE.

HOW TO DEAL WITH A SOUL-SUCKING BREAKUP

The funny thing about writing a book, or one of the funny things at least, is that it takes so long to do it that your perspective can change while you're writing it. You write a book proposal based on things you think you have expertise on, but then your confidence about those topics might change over the months you spend writing the book. That was the case with this chapter. When I wrote this book proposal, I did so from the comfort of a relationship that I very much valued, in a home I shared with my boyfriend that we'd created together. I had been through a painful breakup a few years previous, but I was over that, feeling powerful and strong again.

But life is an asshole sometimes.

While I was writing this book my boyfriend dumped me out of nowhere. I had to move out of the apartment we designed together, the culmination of a lifelong goal I'd had to design a space with someone I loved. Then less than two months later I lost my job. My sense of how much advice I really should be giving on this topic went from about 100 to 0 in the course of a few months. How I felt about myself took a nosedive, I wondered if I should really be writing a book at all. It's a terrible idea to live for outside validation, but we all do it. The blow to my ego of being told I was unlovable and unemployable, simultaneously, was a lethal blow to my self-worth.

We all have experiences like this, but for feelings that are so incredibly universal, they feel unbearably lonely. The biggest challenge I had in writing this book was twofold:

ONE: How to concentrate on such a large project, one which requires endless hours of time spent alone, while your world is crashing down, when you've lost everything you care about—your partner, your job, your home—and have to start over?

TWO: How to give other people advice when you yourself are feeling at your least valuable, your least appealing—anything but an expert? How to meet your deadlines for your advice book when you are feeling so shitty about yourself that you don't think anyone should be following your advice in the first place?

You're probably figuring by now that this is an advice chapter gone awry. I thought I'd have advice for you about how to thrive and move on with your life. But instead all I have to offer are ways to cope until you feel better. The old adage that "time heals all wounds" is true. But that fucking sucks when you are in the depths of a post-breakup depression. The following are my tips for making the most of your depression.

THINK OF IT AS A DEATH

When a partner decides he or she no longer wants to be with you, it can be an incredibly confusing curveball. You go from spending all your time together, to spending all your time alone. It can make you question reality. Life was one thing, then it was something else. So which is it? This new thing or what came before? Was I ever really in love or was I just projecting onto someone else? WHAT IS REAL?

I was having dinner with a friend of mine who told me to view the breakup as a death. I don't want to minimize the suffering of anyone who has lost a partner to an actual death, but losing a partner in any way can feel nearly as violent. One minute they are yours and life feels full, the next they are gone and you feel an enormous void in your heart where they once lived.

Having a friend compare this to death felt like a validation of my pain, it brought me to tears. It made me

feel like I wasn't crazy for feeling such immense sadness. I'd lost the one person I cared most deeply for and it was OK to mourn him as if he were dead.

YOU'RE NOT CRAZY

If you're a hypersensitive person like I am, it's likely you'll have WAY TOO MANY feelings about getting dumped. It's important to keep in mind that these are normal and that you are not crazy for feeling them. People who truly care about other people feel the loss of a partner intensely. Also keep in mind that if you got dumped, it likely had much more to do with your partner and his/her needs/wants/personality. I know exactly why my most recent ex dumped me. I'm not gonna write it here but it had way more to do with him than me. Still hard not to take it personally but makes me feel slightly better that it wasn't my fault.

GET THE FUCK OUT

I've had two significant relationships under my belt and two violently painful breakups to boot. And the only thing that made me feel even a slight bit of solace was getting out of town. I'd drive out to Ojai or Joshua Tree and look around. I'd drive up to Santa Barbara and do some thrift shopping. Or visit family. Each of these trips did nothing to erase any of my sadness over losing my partner. But they did do one thing. They made me remember there was a world out there to enjoy. There was light and beauty. From the depths of depression it can be hard to remember what's good. Forcing yourself out into the world can revive that.

REACH OUT

Post-breakup depression can lead people to sequester themselves inside. I definitely fell into a pattern of sitting at home eating sushi, drinking wine, and crying to movies that totally should not have induced crying (*Clueless*—WHAT?). It can be hard to want to be around other people when your whole being feels like a snotty crying wet raw mess. But it can be the best thing for you. It reminds you that people want to help you. You have a family of friends who want to support you. But in order to get that support you need to reach out and ask for it. Trust me, your friends will be honored you asked for their help. It will make them feel needed and valued and trusted.

DON'T EXPECT TRUE COMFORT TO COME FROM OTHERS

One thing I've noticed in all my wallowing is that there are no magic words anyone can ever say to be truly helpful to other people going through a shitty breakup. Usually it's the opposite—people aren't very reassuring. The best thing you can do as a friend is listen actively by asking questions and reflecting back to the person you're listening to the feelings they're sharing. Your friends won't be able to give you any advice on how to truly get over your sadness. And honestly, friends have a supershort attention span for dealing with sadness.

The lack of interest your friends have in your immense human suffering can be depressing to anyone going through a breakup (or anyone suffering from depression, for that matter). A friend is happy to be confided in about sadness. But most people don't have the ability/interest to hear about it more than once. Your friends don't like hearing about sadness over and over because A) they don't want you to be sad, and B) because they're secretly frustrated they can't just "fix" you immediately, and C) because it's impossible to truly empathize with it. My friend Price Peterson summarized it like this: "Ultimately other people's heartbreak is so boring, and your own is the most important/interesting thing that ever happened." So keep in mind that while you might be enthralled with your own sadness BECAUSE IT'S LITERALLY TAKING OVER YOUR LIFE, it might not seem so fascinating to other people. Ask for help, but don't expect your friends to be saints.

USE YOUR SENSE OF HUMOR AS A COPING MECHANISM

When you are sad, you need your friends. However, being sad can lead to being totally alienating to people, so keep your wits about you; being funny if and when possible will help keep your friends close. I guess this has been a coping mechanism I've used all my life. In painful high school years—maybe even before—when I was targeted for being weird or gay, I often went to a place of humor. I learned over the years it made me appealing. Which is a terrible reason to be funny, deflecting the true pain you feel and making yourself into a clown. But the positive aspect of it is that it makes you take yourself, your struggles, less seriously. It lightens the situation.

GO TO CONCERTS

Some of the best moments since this breakup have been at concerts. I went to see Austra, one of my favorite bands on earth, a few months after I got dumped. The music reached me in a way it might not have had I not been a wound-up ball of emotional vulnerability. Listening to music live, from bands you really love, can be a cathartic experience, can remind you there is beauty that you love in the world.

THE FOUR STAGES OF GAY GRIEF

1. UTTER DISBELIEF

At first, you can't believe what is really happening. You're like, "Wait, what? We were literally just happy yesterday!" It can be really jarring when a relationship ends. For this, I recommend cake. Eat it alone, eat it with your hands, eat it as batter before it's even cooked. You're allowed to eat cake and be bad. This is like the only time you're allowed to eat like a fat fuck and no one is allowed to say anything. Celebrate that. Eat the fuck out of everything. People will be like, "DAM GURL SHE LIVING!" Instead of being like, "Ma'am why u eating so much???" Take advantage of the one privilege you have in this shitty time of your life.

2. DEPTH OF DESPAIR

In this stage of grief you'll have the feeling that everything is terrible and you should just die. DON'T DIE. Resist the urge to stick your head in the oven and cook it like a Thanksgiving turkey! Things will get better and you'll never get revenge on all those people you hate if you die now!

3. ALCOHOLISM

This is clearly the funnest stage of grief because it means you get to drink lots of wine without worrying how many carbs are in it. But it's actually the worst for your emotional well-being. Alcohol is a depressant; depressants make you depressed. Which isn't necessarily a bad thing. A wise old person once said, "The best way out is through." So you kinda have to go through your depression to get to the other side. Scientists agree, wine is the funnest way to up your depression game, so why not indulge a little in this, one of life's inevitable low points?

4. RESIGNED NIHILISM

If I learned one thing from my two long-term relationships it's that everything is meaningless and terrible and nothing matters. The final stage of grief is the realization that your past relationship doesn't matter because life is ultimately a meaningless series of dumb events and that we're just parasites waddling around on a blob of rocks and dirt flying through the middle of outer space. Does your ex matter? No, but neither does anything else. We are just animals and nothing we do makes a difference so we might as well have fun. Wheee.

So there you have it. That's my raw, from-the-middle-of-my-depression take on how you should deal with a breakup, especially for those of you who didn't make the ultimate decision to end the relationship. I don't know if it should make you feel better or worse that I'm literally writing an advice book and I have no idea how to heal whatever pain you might be feeling. What I do know is that writing things down and sharing them with other people can be both cathartic and reassuring.

ABOVE ALL, HONESTY

In my practice as a social media whore and blogger, I've tried to do my best to represent a realistic picture of what my life is, rather than the hyperidealized version many of my lifestyle blogger counterparts do. I do this because I ultimately think that "influencers" do an incredible disservice by pretending our lives are perfect. This tells our readers that their lives, complete with heartache, weight gain, death, job loss, failures, and struggles are somehow inadequate. Yes, there are positive things to concentrate on and when those arise, I share them. But I am also honest about the struggles I face.

In this age of social media bullshit, it can be really hard to share your real feelings about what you are going through with people in your networks, either online or in real time. It's like we don't have the ability to be our true selves anymore, we're too caught up with living up to a fake-ass ideal we see propagated online. But you have no idea how you might help someone by letting your vulnerability come through.

My friend James went through a breakup at a similar time as me and I visited him recently. He explained, through tears, that he was still in a dark spot, in a depression, and that he was struggling. What a gift that was to me, as I was feeling so alone in my grief. So I'll leave you with this: find someone who needs it and open up to them about how you're feeling. You might be helping them much more than you know.

. . . And stop being such a fake-ass bitch on social media.

WHAT TO DO WHEN YOU'VE BEEN LAID OFF AND YOUR LIFE IS RUINED FOREVER

One thing I've learned over my years of professional flailing is that there will inevitably be ups and downs in your career. If you're in a creative field and have taken a considerable number of risks in order to be creatively fulfilled, these ups and downs will be even more pronounced. I live in L.A., and my friends are all artists and weirdos so I see firsthand how difficult it is to make a living in a creative industry.

In all honesty, I never really knew what I wanted to do. When I was in high school, I wanted to be a lawyer. Then after that I wanted to be an art professor. Then after that I wanted to be a graphic designer. Then after that I was like, "FUCK IT I HAVE NO IDEA WHAT I WANT TO DO ANYMORE."

While I didn't know what I wanted "to do" (as in job), I did know what I wanted "to do" (as in actual activities that I liked doing). I knew I wanted to do something where I could use my artistic eye and my ability to skillfully make things by hand. I have always had terrible self-esteem, but one thing I was always confident in was my ability to craft things better than other people. It's so weird, the hardest working people can sometimes be the laziest crafters.

I didn't really ever know I wanted to be an interior designer before it happened. Even though I'd been designing spaces my whole life, I never really considered interior design as a profession until I'd already been cast to play an interior design assistant on an HGTV show. I made that sound random, but I worked hard for that opportunity, essentially working for free in art departments on film/TV sets for years before getting approached to do something on camera. So while my professional development has been a bit random, it's come from a very directed interest I carry—to create beauty.

I get emails all the time from people asking me how to break into the design field. And it's hard for me to respond positively. I think this is a very tough field to really thrive in. In order for me to get where I am, I've essentially had to work for free, get cast on a TV show, and become Internet famous just to get by (keep in mind, I wrote this book at my parents' home, where I lived, as an adult human male). So if you're choosing between being a doctor and being an interior designer, choose medicine. While interior design may seem like it's playing with pillows and screaming "FABULOUS!" at rich women, it's mostly just proposing ideas and waiting for your clients to shit all over them while wondering how you're going to pay your rent next month.

The reason I bring all this up is to let you know, sometimes careers take twists and turns and sometimes you don't know exactly what the end goal is. Obviously, the end goal should be to live a happy life and do the types of activities you like to do. For some people that means taking a job they hate so they can afford to do fun things outside of work. For others it means doing a job they love, even if

it means they never truly have a day off because they're so passionate about what they do. I fall into that latter category, and sometimes I wish I fit into the first because it would be really nice to shut my brain off and forget about work.

I completed graduate school in 2007, during one of the worst economies in modern times. When stuff started going downhill in 2008, I lost my job and wandered around aimlessly for years wondering what to do. I didn't get much help from family during this time, and looking back I'm

kind of shocked that I survived and lived in L.A. the whole time. What this period did for me was give me perspective about my own sense of entitlement. Before this period of joblessness, my multiple Ivy League degrees from multiple Ivy League schools made me believe I should be employable at most entry level places. But rejection after rejection after rejection taught me something about myself: I was literally unemployable and mostly useless. One of my favorite rejections came from Billy's Bakery, a cute bakery around the corner from my apartment in New York, where I was applying to be a cashier. I literally couldn't even land that job. And it wasn't that I was getting turned down for jobs because I was overqualified. I was also getting turned down for jobs I was qualified for (a notable example was a personal assistant position for Jonathan Adler, who took one look at me and screamed GET OUT!*). In my twenties I applied to hundreds of legit jobs (like the type with health insurance, etc.) and I got literally zero of them.

*THIS IS A COMPLETE LIE, BUT I DID APPLY TO WORK THERE AND DIDN'T GET THE JOB.

I'm not telling you this to complain. Just kidding yes I am. Complaining is the best! But I'm also telling you this because I know there are millions of people out there struggling to reach their full potential. Or even just struggling to figure out what the fuck to do with themselves. If my career trajectory has taught me anything, it's that sometimes you work your ass off and get nowhere. Other times you do nothing at all and land an amazing opportunity.

My first big break came in fall 2010, when I was in New York working as a freelance art department bitch (basically a low-level art director for indie films). I came home for a spell after a series of tragedies happened simultaneously. My best friend's father committed suicide in a rather horrifying way and a few weeks later my infant nephew died from a rare undetected heart syndrome called hypoplastic left heart syndrome. I spent so much time coming back to California during that period that I decided it made more sense to move back. Everyone I knew was in a state of darkness and absolutely everything seemed terrible.

Then randomly I applied for an art department job that turned out to be an on-camera position to play Emily Henderson's assistant in the TV show she had won on a reality show called *Design Star*. Talk about luck and happenstance. My entire career changed because someone else won a reality show, which in and of itself is an incredible feat, making it past all those rounds of casting, navigating through the challenges and politics of the TV show's production—pretty fucking crazy if you think about it. My whole career changed because some random person I didn't know won a reality show, then I got to be on the show she won because a casting person in Canada liked me.

In the end, it wasn't the straight A's I got in college, or that I graduated early, or that I started working when I was fourteen all the way through college that ended up making me successful. It was that my face and personality were appealing to a casting director I'd never met before. Ironic, because I've always hated my face and personality.

I PROMISE THERE IS A POINT TO THIS I'M NOT JUST HUMBLEBRAGGING AND WHINING.

I guess my point is that we only have so much control in our success or lack thereof. You can beat yourself up all you want about not being where you want to be career-wise, financially, etc., but ultimately so much of success is about being in the right place at the right time. Alternatively, this means if you're successful you have to realize your success is the result of a lot of luck. It's not just because you toiled all alone against the world. If you've made it, you had privileges, whether they be innate to who you are or related to how, where, and with what advantages you were raised. So successful people, you can get off your high horse. And underachievers, it's not your fault. SO STOP BEATING YOURSELF UP ALREADY. You're doing a great job!

WHY BLAME YOURSELF WHEN YOU CAN BLAME OTHER PEOPLE?

Here's the truth, if you've gotten laid off it's likely not your fault. Don't blame yourself. Blaming yourself will only lead to lower self-esteem, which will only lead to a longer period of unemployment, which will lead to even lower self-esteem. You should first start with blaming other people. Was it your boss' fault for being a dick? Was it the fault of a past Republican president who deregulated the banks so much they went crazy and started predatory lending that imploded the economy?

If you're anything like me, you probably spend most of your time blaming yourself for everything. So a layoff is the perfect time to take a break from that and blame everyone else. You know who gets ahead in this world? LOUD BLOWHARDS WHO SCREAM THEIR WAY INTO EVERY ROOM AND DON'T QUESTION THEMSELVES. If you look at most CEOs, they're all sociopaths with narcissistic

personality disorder. Maybe the reason you got laid off is that you weren't loud enough about how awesome you are, causing your former boss to forget. If you'd spent more time blaming other people for your mistakes and less time wondering if you were doing something wrong, you'd probably still have a job.

TELL YOUR FRIENDS HOW YOU FEEL

You know what makes everything better? Sitting at a restaurant whining to your friends. When they get tired of your whining, just ask them a question about themselves to keep them engaged. Then, once they've started responding, figure out a way to steer the conversation back to you and your problems.

I've found over my countless failures as an adult that being honest and open about my setbacks is not only helpful in dealing with my personal shame, it's also helpful to the people around me because they, too, have struggled at times in their lives. There's nothing worse than people who run around pretending everything is perfect all the

time. With people like that, you just wanna scream, "BE A PERSON!" Being vulnerable allows people to help you and also lets them know to think of you if they hear of any job opps. Remember, most jobs are obtained through networking, so as much whining as you can muster is good for your job prospects.

THINK ABOUT WHAT'S REALLY IMPORTANT: YOU!

If there's ever a time in your life to concentrate on yourself and your own improvement, it's during a layoff. While losing a job may cause you to lose one thing (money), it causes you to gain something that is equally valuable (time). How you spend that time determines how successful your layoff will be. The first time I was laid off, during the great recession of 2009, I decided to use my spare time pursuing my interests, interning in different TV/film art department jobs. This mindless exploration ultimately led me to my job on HGTV, which has led to my job as a famous rich person interior designer to the stars. Using my free time to really think about what I wanted to do, and make myself available to do it, ultimately led me to where I wanted to go.

WRITE IT DOWN

If you are reading this book, you probably know that I love writing things down and sharing my thoughts with anyone who will listen. For years, I've been blogging about my life and things that interest me. I find that sharing my hopes, fears, happiness, and sadness with people gives me a feeling of purpose in times where everything seems meaningless. During a layoff, you are in one of life's low periods. This doesn't mean you need to hide. Sharing your interests, sadness, and fears with other people will be therapeutic for you and let everyone else know they are not alone in their interests, sadness, and fears. You help other people by being honest about what worries you. Obviously, you have to keep a balance, your whole life can't just be complaining. But you shouldn't feel like you need to hide your struggles in order to be liked. That's not how humanity works. People want to help each other. People want to help you and hear you and lift you up.

I HATE YOUR WEDDING

WE'RE NOT FRIENDS, WHY IS THIS HAPPENING?

Somehow you've gotten invited to a wedding for people you don't care about and you're either too lazy or too polite to decline their invite. Below are my tips on what to do when someone awful invites you to his or her wedding.

YOUR DRESS LOOKS LIKE EVERY OTHER GODDAMN WEDDING DRESS

Ma'am. I have to tell you something. Your wedding dress looks exactly like every other goddamn wedding dress I've ever seen. I know this may come as a shock. But it's true. So stop running around being like, "You know, I just really wanted a dress that would be special. I was so excited when I found this one. Because it's really unique, you know?" And I'm like, "NO I DON'T KNOW BECAUSE IT LOOKS LIKE A CARBON COPY OF EVERY FUCKING WEDDING DRESS THAT HAS EVER EXISTED."

Here's the deal, I don't hate weddings. Weddings are a ceremony and I actually think we don't have enough ceremonies left in this day and age. I love going all out for holidays, graduations, etc. I just don't like it when people pretend that tired-ass shit is brand new. Lady, your wedding dress is white and fluffy. It looks like every other motherfucking wedding dress I've ever seen. Now if you had come down the aisle dressed as Björk in that swan dress, I would have stood up and clapped so hard my hands would have been pulverized into bloody stumps. But your dress looks like every other fucking wedding dress ever. So don't come screaming into my face about how it's the most original dress that ever happened. It's not.

And Gays, don't even get me started. Why are the grooms dressed like twins? OK fine that's kinda hot or whatever, BUT GROSS. I know most of you are just trying to marry carbon copies of yourself but you have to at least pretend that's not the case on your wedding day.

I'M LITERALLY SO DISAPPOINTED IN ALL OF YOU. This is your own day to go batshit crazy wearing couture FREAKY clothing and you're wearing the same thing everyone has been wearing to weddings since the beginning of time? For my wedding, my husband and I are both going to dress like Disney princes. Like not because I'm a Disney weirdo or anything but because I think that would be hilarious and would freak everyone out. I'd be Beast (but like at the end where he's hot) and he could be Aladdin. So cute.

BACHELOR(ETTE) PARTIES ARE WEIRD FOR GAY PEOPLE

Something that no one ever talks about is that bachelor and bachelorette parties are weird as fuck for gays. Why? Because as chill and cool as you are, they always end up turning into a scenario in which stereotypical heteronormative identity is assumed. Like if I'm at a bachelor party for a straight dude, for example, how am I supposed to respond to this stripper? THIS IS SO AWKWARD. And bachelorette parties can be even worse. If you're the gay guy friend, you are always the only one and are constantly referred to as ONE OF THE LADIES. Which is fine because many gay guys, myself included, don't have a lot of hang-ups about being referred to using feminine pronouns. HOWEVER, that gets kinda old.

Here's the deal, America! We have to all start just being like the people in the liberal Northern California pocket I come from. We don't do gendered bachelor(ette) parties

and baby showers. We just invite everyone and it's way less weird. This way, the gay people you know won't feel like total weirdos for being at a bachelorette party and also dads-to-be don't have to be left out of the fun of baby showers. EVERYONE WINS!

PLEASE DON'T PLAY "I LIKE BIG BUTTS" AT YOUR RECEPTION

In a scientific study of weddings, researchers found that 98.7 percent of all people born between the years 1970 and 1990 played the song "I Like Big Butts" at their wedding. It's also been found that 99 percent of the wedding attendants responded in the exact same way, by looking at each other, widening their eyes, and going, "OOOOOOH SHIT! They went there!" You see, when this song is played you're supposed to be slightly scandalized but also amused. You're supposed to be like, "THIS IS A FANCY PROPER WEDDING AND THEY'RE PLAYING THIS COMPLETELY INAPPROPRIATE SONG! HOW IS IT POSSIBLE FOR THESE TWO REALITIES TO COEXIST?" Which is what you think the first time you hear it at a wedding. But the thirtieth time you hear it at a wedding, the only natural response is ALL WHITE PEOPLE ARE THE SAME AND I HATE THEM.

Don't be like all the other white people. Don't play "I Like Big Butts" at your wedding. Please.

I BOUGHT YOU THIS BUT I DIDN'T WANT TO

The only thing worse than going to a wedding you don't want to go to for people you secretly (or not so secretly) hate is buying a present for those people. You can't show up empty-handed, so the best thing to do is just buy the cheapest thing on their registry and put it in a huge box with lots of bricks so it looks like something they're really going to like. Then, when they open it they'll be as disappointed in their gift as you are in them as human beings.

HOW TO MASK YOUR HATRED OF THE WEDDING YOU'RE AT

I'm not sure how you got yourself into this mess, but you're at a wedding you don't want to be at. How are you going to deal with this?

1. Roll your eyes

2. Defend your personal space by liberally deploying RBF (Resting Bitch Face)

3. Troll the pre-wedding photo shoot

4. Drink a lot

DO YOU HATE YOUR FRIENDS?

A GUIDE TO FIGURING IT OUT

I didn't have a lot of friends growing up. This is something a lot of people love to say, especially people like me who are writers or actors or other creative types. I'm not sure why this narrative is true, but it is. People who were big ol' losers as kids tend to have more to say as grown-ups.

Their stories are more relatable, their hearts humbler. Someone who was popular as a kid rarely achieves success. But my impression is that most people who end up being successful as grown-ups struggled in their youth with loneliness.

What loneliness did for me is give me the solitude to make things by myself. My family didn't have television (by choice) while I was growing up, so my free time was spent playing games alone, drawing things, making fantasy homes out of Legos, and making elaborate fashion sketches, mostly of ridiculous dresses. It is my firm belief that the hours, days, and years I spent alone as a kid, making things, playing, and imagining are the reason I became a creative adult. What I'm saying is that having friends is overrated. You get so much more done without them.

As a kid, I was cripplingly shy. My mom used to give me money to buy whatever I wanted at the store with one caveat: I had to go to the cashier and pay for it myself. To this day, just thinking about this gives me anxiety. I was so shy, so worried I'd say something wrong or stupid. What is it that is so terrifying about strangers?

I grew up with the same fourteen kids in my class my whole life until I went to high school in a neighboring town in a school FILLED WITH STRANGERS. Naturally, I was terrified. But over my years there I somehow learned to mask my shyness and pretend to be a popular person. I was friends with a lot of the popular kids, so it was an easy role to play.

To a certain extent, I think that's still what I do. I have a considerable amount of social anxiety, but people who meet me tend to think I'm outgoing and gregarious. I guess the tip here is fake it till you make it. Pretending not to be terrified of people is the first step in making friends. But what if the friends you make are assholes? In this section we're going to chat about how to tell if your friends are dicks and what to do if they are.

SIGNS YOUR FRIENDS ARE DICKS

THEY LOOK AT THEIR PHONES MORE THAN THEY LOOK AT YOU

If your friends can't be present enough to give you the attention you deserve, you should consider dumping them immediately. But first, give them a warning. I had a friend who used to spend the entirety of our lunches on his phone. So one day I was all, "Do you realize that you've been staring at your phone the whole time we've been at lunch?" And he was like, "No, oh my god!" And then he stopped. That friend's name is Nathan Carden and I'd like to take this moment to publicly shame him within the print of this book for ignoring me at all those lunches. LET THIS BE A LESSON TO PEOPLE EVERYWHERE THAT IF YOU STARE AT YOUR PHONES MORE THAN AT YOUR FRIENDS ONE DAY A FRIEND WILL WRITE A BOOK ABOUT HOW AWFUL YOU ARE AND EVERYONE WILL BE MAD AT YOU.

THEY'RE ALWAYS GANGING UP ON YOU

Do your friends hang out together when you're gone and devise plots to ostracize you? Do they secretly poison potential partners against you by telling them you're crazy and lack basic human empathy? Do they spend their weekends thinking of ways to make sure you'll never work in this town again? Probably. Which means it's time to say goodbye to them forever.

THEY SAY THINGS ABOUT YOU BEHIND YOUR BACK

If you find out your friends are talking about you behind your back, saying unsavory things, you should immediately say something equally unsavory to twice as many people. This will start a chain reaction in which everyone is talking shit about everyone else. And honestly that's what the world deserves if there is even one person saying even one bad thing about you (even if it's true).

THEY ONLY CARE ABOUT APPEARANCES

There are certain friends who are only friends with you because they think you can do something for them. Let's face it, you're totally cool and everyone wants to be friends with you. But occasionally a superficial person might seek out your friendship for the sole purpose of upping their social status. A friend like this isn't loyal, and will drop you the second your social standing comes into question. Test your friends to make sure they're not like this by creating fake scenarios in which you need help. Call them and be like, "HELP! I'm trapped at the mall because someone stole my car keys while I was talking to a hot guy!" And see if they come get you. If your friend does not pass these tests, it's time to say goodbye.

YOU HATE YOUR FRIENDS, NOW WHAT?

So now that we've established that your friends are terrible, let's chat about how we're going to turn your life around and get you the posse you deserve. In order to seek out new friends, first you need to determine what really matters in a friendship. Since you're so busy, I've already done that for you and I'm going to list it below.

LOYALTY

Will this friend kill for you? If so, maybe move on. That's going a bit far, don't you think? But you do want to seek out friends who will actually stick by you through thick and thin. In order to assess their ability to stick by you no matter what, it's important to conduct experiments that test their loyalty. Pretend you're falling off a bridge and if they come over to catch you that means they are a loyal and true friend.

GENEROSITY

I think of myself as a very generous friend and consider my friends to be very generous as well. To test whether they make the grade in the generosity department, dress like an old beggar woman and hide in the bushes outside their house. When they come outside be like, "PLEASE SIR CAN I HAVE AN APPLE?" And if they say yes that's how you know they are kind and giving and worthy of your friendship.

SMARTS

You can't have conversations with friends who are dumb as rocks, so it's important to test your friend's intellect before deciding on whether you can be besties. Show them a foreign film. If they respond, "WHY WERE THEM PEOPLE TALKIN' SO FUNNY?" then they're probably not friend material. A smart friend values people from different cultures.

FUNNESS

One of the most important parts of friendship is having fun. The easiest way to tell if someone is fun or not is to hand them a glow stick at night. A fun person will immediately start dancing and waving it around in the air. A boring person will be like, "What is this?"

DIFFERENT FRIENDS MEET DIFFERENT ENDS

Like a fine wine, you are complex and filled with quirks that make you YOU. Just like you are a complex potpourri of character traits, your group of friends is also a complex mix of characters. Thus, not all your friends can be best friends. Different friends for different occasions, I always say. There are friends to go to the symphony with and friends to go dancing with. And often they're not the same friends. Not everyone can be as well rounded as you. So in seeking out friends, it's OK if they don't tick off all your interest boxes. NO ONE IS PERFECT (except you).

IF YOU'RE TRYING NOT TO BE A CRAZY HERMIT, YOU GOTTA GET OUT THERE

No one ever made friends by staying home being a nerd. Every friend I've made as an adult has been at a party, art opening, public event (like jazz in the park or whatever. DON'T JUDGE ME. Yes, jazz is lame but that's not the point of jazz in the park. THE POINT IS DRINKING WINE OUTSIDE, DUH!). My point is that as many apps and online groups as there are, the best way to make actual friends is in person. When my parents moved to a new community upon retirement, my mom immediately joined a gardening organization where she made all of her new friends. Well, all but one, whom she stole from my aunt, who deserved it because she's not good at sharing.

YOU DON'T NEED NO MAN

Here's the deal. Friends make everything better. But the most important friend in your life is YOU. So while it's good to seek out people to share you life with, it's best to do it from a place of self-confidence. You can entertain yourself, and doing stuff alone is cooler than doing stuff with friends. But friends are the icing on the cake. So don't be so thirsty for friends that you just befriend any jerk that shows up. Be selective with who you let into your life while also keeping an open mind to the fact that the friends you make might not fit into the neat boxes for them you've created in your head.

NOW GO MAKE SOME FRIENDS, K?

DO IT YOURSELF

Did you know that people who know how to make things themselves will be the last to die in the apocalypse? I did. And that's why I've spent my life perfecting my crafting skills, awaiting the day these skills will come in handy and save my life (and maybe even all of humanity). This chapter will teach you to make some of my favorite home decor crafts in seven easy do-it-yourself (DIY) projects. Don't feel like making anything yourself? Watch me do it! There's nothing more fun than sitting back and watching someone else work.

HOW TO MAKE YOUR OWN ORBLANDO OUT OF HARDWARE STORE GARBAGE

The television series that launched my design career, *Secrets from a Stylist* (RIP), was one of the best, most stressful experiences of my life. While on camera, I was basically acting like a silly idiot next to Emily Henderson, off camera I was driving all over town like an actual lunatic trying to find furniture and accessories for the homes we made over on each week's episode. The concept of this show was that each home received two makeovers, which required a lot of sourcing each week in addition to all the shooting that was required. But it was always fun because we'd put a rug down and be like, "that was so easy!" while in reality we'd basically killed ourselves to find the right rug in time for the shot. TV is lies, people. Don't let anyone tell you different. Especially design shows.

My favorite thing about working with Emily is that she trusted me and was open to my ideas. On one episode, when I had the idea to make a wire chandelier, she went for it. We were reaching the end of the season and running out of budget, but we needed a large-scale light fixture to go over a giant dining table in an even more giant living room/dining room combo space. I had to work on this guy every day after getting home from shooting/sourcing all day. The result was a relatively inexpensive, one-of-a-kind light fixture. I named him ORBLANDO. Get it?

HOW TO MAKE IT!

What You'll Need

+ 14-gauge galvanized wire (I used about 150 feet [45 m] for this 24-inch [60 cm] orb)

+ Narrow-gauge galvanized wire (sometimes referred to as floral wire)

+ Chain or wire for hanging the Orb from the ceiling

+ Light kit (you can buy these for plug-in ceiling fixtures)

+ Needle nose pliers

+ G40 light bulb (or other large light bulb)

+ Spray paint (optional)

STEP 1: Make Hoops

✦ First, make three wire hoops (from the 14-gauge wire) in the size you want your Orblando to be. For example, if you want a pendant that is 2 feet (60 cm) wide, make a wire hoop that is 2 feet wide. This wire is thin and easy to work with, but not necessarily sturdy. You'll need to double up the first three loops so they're strong enough to support the rest of the wires.

STEP 2: Create Armature

✦ Using the floral wire, attach the first three hoops together. Speaking of hoops, remember how Jennifer Lopez used to wear hoop earrings all the time and now she doesn't? I miss that. As far as creating the armature for the fixture goes, it's like you're making a very simple globe shape from these three hoops. It doesn't have to be perfect because you're going to add like five thousand more layers of wire.

STEP 3: Finesse Your Weave!

✦ Remember Sigourney Weaver in *Aliens*? Well, for this part of the DIY, pretend that your name is [Insert Your Name] Weaver and that your job is to weave and weave and weave 14-gauge wire together until your Orb looks like a giant spherical scribble. The most important part of the weaving process is that whenever the 14-gauge wire intersects, you attach it together with a 3-inch (7.6 cm) piece of the thinner wire (just wrap the thin wire around and point all the ends inward so they don't cut anyone). This sounds easy, but it gets SUPER tedious because there are so many intersections. If you don't bind your intersections the Orb won't be structurally sound, so it's the most important part of the process.

STEP 4: Test Its Strength

✦ Keep weaving until your Orblando is as lacy and complicated as the front of a wig on *RuPaul's Drag Race*. Make sure to leave an opening near the top big enough for the G40 bulb to fit through. To test if your Orb is strong enough, try bouncing it on the floor (or any scratch-proof surface, preferably outside). If it can maintain it's shape after a light bounce it's probably strong enough to hang (if it's too weak it will eventually start to sag like my face).

STEP 5: Pick a Color

+ Before you hang your Orblando, choose a color to spray it (and your hardware) and do so in a protected outdoor area. You can leave your Orb raw, but know that it will probably not stay that bright silver color forever (it dulls a bit over time).

STEP 6: Attaching the Orb

+ If you have a light kit with a chain, you can attach the Orb directly to the chain. If you used a simple cord like I used, you'll need to attach your Orb either to the canopy with hanging wire (make sure to tape if off inside) or to the ceiling using hooks.

MAKE YOUR OWN GODDAMN COFFEE TABLE

WHY'D YA MAKE YER OWN COFFEE TABLE?

Through the ages, man has asked himself the time-honored question, "Should I make my own goddamn coffee table or go to a big-box store and buy one made of melamine and wood with chemicals known to cause cancer?" And the booming answer from God Himself has always been, "MAKE YOUR OWN GODDAMN COFFEE TABLE." Surely if God Himself takes his own name in vain to describe the importance of making your own coffee table, it must be a pretty important thing.

I've always made things myself. Partially because I wanted to and partially because no one bought me as many presents as I thought I deserved. One of my favorite phrases growing up was, "HEY CAN YOU HELP ME WITH THIS NO OK FINE I'LL DO IT MYSELF." It was my passive-aggressive way (or maybe just aggressive way) of telling the world I didn't need anyone to help me, I will figure it out myself IF IT KILLS ME.

Lots of people think DIY projects are for wimpy homebodies who have nothing better to do than make their houses pretty. Those people are wrong. DIY people are going to be the last people to die in the impending apocalypse. We will be crafting our own boats as the oceans rise, paddling away as you store-bought people drown in the ocean and we fake-smilingly look down at you saying, "Maybe you should have learned a thing or two about making things yourself."

DOING IT YOURSELF IS VERY IMPORTANT

As God Himself said in the previous paragraph, doing it yourself is very important. First, because it can save you some money. Second, because it's a way of impressing houseguests and potential mates. Say you bring a date home for a glass of wine. If you set your glasses of wine down on a boring store-bought coffee table, they'll look at you like, "Oh, this (wo)man goes to the store and buys things. LIKE A GODDAMN BABY." But if you happen to scream-whisper into their ear, "I MADE THIS MYSELF" as you set the glasses of wine down, they might be like, "Oh wow! This (wo)man will be able to provide for me and my future family and is undoubtedly skilled at lovemaking, fishing, and will be able to carry me in his/her arms if a fire erupts because of our intensely heated passion."

This is why it's SO important to tell people you've made things yourself. Don't just tell them politely. Yell it directly at their faces as they walk in the door. Any guest will be impressed not only by the power of your fabrication skills, but also by the strength of your vocal cords. The only thing more important than making things yourself is telling literally everyone on earth that you have done so.

WHAT IS A COFFEE TABLE AND WHY?

Lots of people don't get why we need coffee tables. They ask me all the time, "Why do I need a coffee table? I don't even drink coffee in my living room!" My response is always the same: "GOD MADE ADAM AND EVE NOT ADAM AND

STEVE!" This normally throws them off for a minute while I think of my real answer. Which is that you need a coffee table because having a coffee table is the only thing that separates us from the animals (well, that and cleaning the house) and if we don't have one we may as well be in cages at the zoo because what order is there in the world if you can't find a place to put your glass/bottle of pinot grigio while you sit on the sofa diligently watching *Degrassi: Next Class*? Get It Together, accept that you need a coffee table, and choose another issue to pester me about. I ONLY HAVE SO MUCH TIME ON THIS PLANET AND I DON'T PLAN ON SPENDING IT YELLING AT YOU ABOUT WHY YOU NEED A COFFEE TABLE.

For those of you who don't know, a coffee table is a low, wide table where people put books they never read that they only bought to look fancy/cultured/like they know how to read. It's likely that this book will one day end up on your coffee table and for that I'm thankful. This means I'm helping trick people into thinking you are smarter, cooler, and more literate than you really are. And my basic goal in life is tricking people into thinking I and the people around me are way less garbage-y than we really are. If this book makes it onto your coffee table, you've made it. We're in this together and no one will ever find out how terrible/trashy we really are! Hashtag winning!

HOW TO MAKE IT!

What you'll need:

- 4 pieces of 48 x 7 x ¾ inch (102 x 17.8 1.9 cm) wood for the tabletop
- 2 pieces of 25 x 2 x ¾ inch (63.5 x 5 x 1.9 cm) wood for the crossbars
- 12 pieces of 16 x 5 x ¾ inch (40.6 x 12.7 x 1.9 cm) wood for table legs
- 10 brass "L" brackets
- Four 1½ inch (3.8 cm) side-facing "L" brackets
- Fifty 1¼ inch (3.1 cm) wood screws

STEP 1: Tabletop

- Mark a line perpendicular to the long side of the 48-inch (102 cm) piece of wood 12 inches (30 cm) from each end (1a). Lay the long pieces of wood next to each other and attach the crossbars on top of the marked line (25 x 2-inch [63 x 5 cm] wood pieces) using your wood screws (1b). Set the tabletop aside.

STEP 2: Table Legs

- Attach two 16 x 5-inch (40.6 x 12.7 cm) wood pieces together into an "L" shape with brass "L" brackets as shown in the image (2a). Make sure to predrill holes before attempting to screw them together so it's not impossible to get the screws in (2b). Use a drill bit just slightly smaller than the screws to create the predrilled holes (2c). Repeat six times until you have six wood Ls.

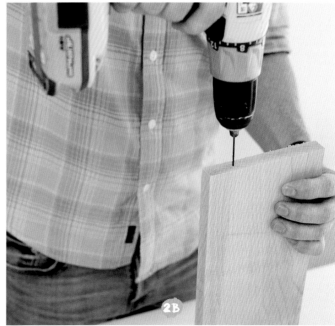

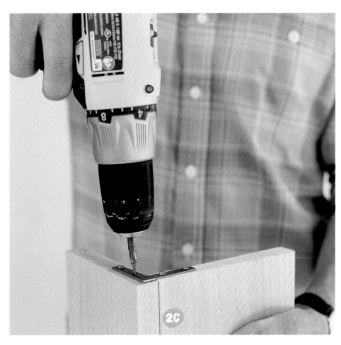

STEP 3: Accordions

→ Using the remaining "L" brackets, attach three of these L-shaped leg pieces together into an accordion pattern. Then do it again with the remaining three L-shaped leg pieces, for a separate, second set of accordion legs. Measure roughly 3 inches (7.6 cm) from the edge of the tabletop to the outermost accordion point on each side, where you will attach the table legs.

STEP 4: Attaching the Tabletop

Attach the table legs to the tabletop using side-facing "L" brackets and wood screws. Attach the brackets so that they're facing inward and not on the outer, more visible edges. With the help of a friend (if you have one), turn the table over and admire your handiwork!

COFFEE TABLE RULES

I'm basically a teenager hiding under the bleachers smoking pot while talking about how shitty rules, adults, and conformity are, but that doesn't mean I hate all rules. Below are some rules for coffee tables THAT MUST NOT BE DISOBEYED.

1. You have to have a coffee table, no matter where you live or what you do for a living. There is no escaping this. It has been decreed by God Himself.

2. Your coffee table should be 18 inches (45 cm) from your sofa and other furniture. If it's too close, it may chop your legs off (which would be completely your fault, therefore making it impossible to get any pity from anyone in your life, therefore negating the fun of having an injury).

3. Coffee tables should be slightly shorter, slightly higher, or the same height as your sofa/chair seat height. If your guests come in and see a too-short coffee table or an insanely high coffee table they are going to freak out and know immediately that you are garbage.

4. You should put stuff on your coffee table. Not too little and not too much. For this, you're going to need A LOT of coffee table books. Even if you don't know how to read, these are imperative. The best coffee table book is this one, and it's likely you'll need 60–100 copies of it to make your table look good (and I'm not just saying that because I live under a hobbit bridge right now and could def use the money).

5. You should always have a vase with tall flowers on your coffee table. This tells your guests, "I was raised with money and can play the piano." If you don't put flowers on your coffee table, it will tell your guests, "I was raised by animals, and not even cool animals like gazelles or owls, but barbarian animals like raccoons who do nothing but steal trash and scratch people when confronted."

APPROPRIATE ITEMS TO PLOP ONTO YOUR HOMEMADE COFFEE TABLE

1. Books (this one, over and over)

2. Overpriced, small-batch scented candles

3. Low, wide ceramic bowls that cost more than you make annually

4. Family photos

5. Empty boxes (as a metaphor for your empty soul)

6. Bowls of those pastel-colored, candy-covered almonds. Just kidding.

7. No, wait, actually I was serious about those candy almonds. They're so good.

8. I'm fat.

NOW THAT YOU'VE LEARNED YOUR LESSON

Now that you've learned the necessity of making your own coffee table, go forth and do so. You'll notice this coffee table is, like myself, imperfect. The tabletop has a bit of a Wabi-sabi look to it, meaning it's uneven and a bit rustic. I'd explain more to you about Wabi-sabi, but I'm not here to give you a history lesson, I'm here to be your friend and tell you you're doing it wrong. Just remember, your ability to do things yourself will help you during the End of Timez. Someday, you'll thank me for this. You're welcome.

A BASIC TRAY TO IMPRESS YOUR FRIENDS WHO ARE ALSO BASIC

Trays are one the most essential design objects that most people forget they need. I'm not quite sure why this is, but I'd like to put a stop to it right this very moment! Trays are basically rugs for your tabletop. Meaning they do the same thing a rug does for an overall space. They corral objects and create order. They define a space upon a tabletop surface where you can place decorative items, books, and other knickknacks. A world without trays would be a world of chaos and destruction. A world of overwhelming conflict and strife. But a world with trays is a world of peace and order. Which world do you choose?

I think if you're reading this book you're probably the type of person who likes tabletop styling. Meaning you like objects in your house, you like the eclectic look and the visual interest it creates. I'm assuming this because this is something I include in almost all of my design work and if that's untrue I don't know how you got in here and quite frankly I don't appreciate you showing up to my party just to question my authority. The reason I bring up tabletop styling is that trays are an essential part of creating table and shelf-scapes that look organized and attractive. A vignette with trays is how you look as you head out for a night on the town with your ladies. A vignette without trays is what you look like at 3 a.m. after you've been drinking for five hours. Does this clear everything up for you?

I'm assuming the reason that most people are tray-less is due to the price of trays. I hear you on that one. One of my favorite pastimes is waddling around the tray store screaming at the sales associates, "$100? For this? IT'S A SLAB OF WOOD!" I know it's not the sales associate's fault the tray is so expensive, but that rage has to go somewhere, right? Today I'm going to share a trick with you that will change your life forever. Making a tray is supereasy and you can do it yourself. No more screaming at sales associates. Now you can just yell at yourself while you craft!

HOW TO MAKE IT!

What You'll Need:

+ Wood cut to size at a hardware store
+ For this tray, I used pine in the following sizes:
+ Base: 12 x 15 x ¾ inches (30 x 38 x 1.9 cm)
+ Side pieces: 2 x 15 x ¾ inches (5 x 38 x 1.9 cm)
+ End pieces: 2 x 10½ x ¾ inches (5 x 26.6 x 1.9 cm)

(When figuring out the size of your pieces, remember to subtract the thickness of the wood from the length of the two end pieces. Since my wood was ¾ inches (1.9 cm) thick, I subtracted 1½ inches (1.2 cm) so the pieces would be flush with the base.)

+ Wood glue
+ Medium-grain sand paper
+ Stain-ready wood filler
+ Putty knife
+ Wood stain

STEP 1: Make Someone Else Do the Hard Part

One of the best tricks I've learned in my years designing is "WHY DO THINGS YOURSELF YOU CAN MAKE OTHER PEOPLE DO?" I use this philosophy in much of my DIY exploration. For this project, I just waddled into a hardware store that sells wood and asked them to cut it all to the specific sizes I needed for my project. I did this for a few reasons: A) I don't have a woodshop in my house and cutting these pieces would have been way harder for me than for the dude at the store who knows how to use power tools, and B) I'm scared of chopping my fingers off my body. Most big hardware stores, including one that rhymes with DOME KEEPO, will cut wood to any size you want. The sad part is they usually won't cut mitered (45-degree angle) corners, so your DIY projects are confined to ones you can do with straight cuts.

You can totally cut the pieces necessary for this project yourself if you have the right tools. But before you do so, ask yourself if you're really willing to risk cutting off all your arms and legs just to make a tray. I mean, trays are great, but are they worth that?

STEP 2: Sand

When wood is cut, the edges tend to be jagged and rough, like my face the day after a party where I drank too many Cosmopolitans. Just kidding, I don't drink those. OR DO I?

Sand the edges of all your wood pieces so they won't look as scary as my face. For pine, I like to use a medium-grit sandpaper and finish off with a finer grit. But it's really up to you how gritty you want to get. Remember, the larger the grit on your sandpaper the roughest the finish on the wood will be. If you're going for a smooth finish, start with a larger grit and progress to a smaller one.

STEP 3: Glue

I hate using tools when I don't have to. So I made this a no-nail project. And by "nails" I mean the kind you hammer, not the kind you buy in a box and press onto your existing lame nails using a toxic glue you can get high on. Use a wood glue for this part and apply it liberally, keeping paper towels handy in case you get glue on your press-ons.

STEP 4: Add Side Pieces

In modern times, a "Side Piece" usually refers to a lady/man you keep on the side to have affairs with when you feel like it. It's a very morally dubious thing to be. But this is a clean-cut book for families (kinda) so the side piece we're

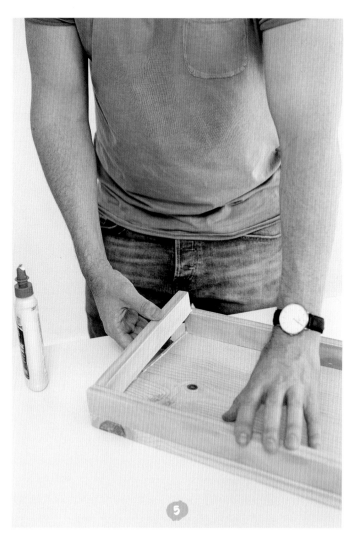

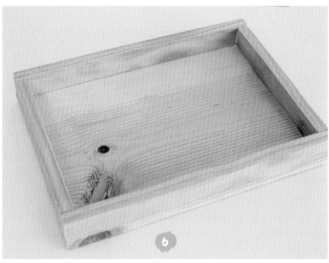

talking about today is wholesome, sweet, and helpful. This side piece will create the sides of our tray. Press these firmly into place while thinking about what this side piece means to you and how it might be your only true chance at love and partnership. Wipe away excess glue.

STEP 5: Place End Pieces at the End of the Tray

Before you insert the end pieces make sure to put glue on them. Shocker, these End Pieces go on the end of the tray! Smash them down with your human fists so they bond strongly to the other wood pieces.

STEP 6: Watch That Shit Dry!

This part is boring. You're just waiting for the wood glue to dry. During this time you could attempt an activity. Like you could go work out or go to the mall with a friend to talk about guys. It takes about five hours for it to get completely dry.

STEP 7: Wood Filler

Even if you've clamped your wood tightly together, there are bound to be gaps between the different components of your tray. Make sure they look seamless by using wood filler to close those gaps.

STEP 8: Stain

I chose a stain finish for this tray. You can also leave it bare, seal it with mineral oil, or paint it a solid color. I like the stain because it maintains some earthiness. The way most stains work is you paint on a thick layer, let it stand for a few seconds, and wipe it away (follow the instructions on the can, that was literally the laziest garbage-instructions I've ever given anyone).

STEP 9: Enjoy You Handiwork!

You did it! You made a tray by forcing someone to cut wood for you then gluing it together! Once it's dry, you can use your tray for a number of activities. Try using it to carry glasses out to a delighted party. Try using it as a raft for your hampsters in the bathtub! Try putting it on your coffee table filled with baby doll heads! The possibilities are endless! And now that you know you can make a tray, you know you can do anything. YOU GO GIRL!

I'M ASHAMED OF THIS SHITTY DIY

You guys, I think it's been well established by this point in the book that I am not perfect. I am a human being and I fuck up all the time. As in the planning, photographing, and writing of this book! I am including one of these huge mistakes here for everyone to see. It might seem weird for an author being published by a major publisher to include such a glaring fuck-up in his very first book, but I'm doing it for a reason.

A big component of design—DIY projects in particular—is experimentation. And when you're experimenting, mistakes come with the territory. People who experiment are innovators and culture creators, style makers. They are the bloggers, influencers, writers, actors, and artists who we all look up to, who make us feel shitty about ourselves because they're so cool. People who don't experiment are followers, cookie-cutter lemmings who fail to be memorable. Which do you want to be? Do you want to just wait for things to be trendy and popular enough that you can find them at your local garbage store? Or do you want to be the type of person who tries new things and occasionally makes mistakes?

LET US ALL BE THE TYPE OF FOOLS WHO AREN'T AFRAID TO MAKE MISTAKES.

When I planned this project, I thought, "Hey, Self, you know what's cute? Rope doorstops!" So I decided to make one using items I found at the hardware store. What followed was one of the most grueling and humiliating experiences of my entire life. Worse than the time I was seven and I threw a pumpkin-carving party and invited my whole class, but then Ashley Ronnell decided to throw a pumpkin-carving party the same night and everyone went to her party instead. Actually, it's not worse than that. FUCK YOU ASHLEY RONNELL!

I'm sharing this DIYFAIL story with you in the hopes that it'll teach you a very valuable lesson about DIY and life in general. You're never going to get anywhere if you don't take some chances. And, yes, this means sometimes you're going to fuck up royally and everyone will laugh at you. But the alternative is to be so crippled by fear that you never try anything. I am working with a client right now who has been so worried he'll make the wrong design choices that he's lived in a superexpensive apartment without furniture FOR OVER A YEAR. This man is a fancy Hollywood executive. And his fear of fucking up has kept him from having a goddamn sofa. HE HAS NOWHERE TO SIT BECAUSE OF HIS FEARS. Don't be like him! Be like me! Make mistakes then write about them in your book so literally millions of people can read about it.

So yeah, that's my explanation for why I'm keeping this ugly-ass DIY in my multiplatinum, Oscar-nominated, destined-to-be-a-classic book. You're welcome!

HOW TO MAKE IT!

What You'll Need:

+ Literally zero taste
+ 1 garden edging brick
+ 1 cork plant pad (designed to absorb moisture under planters)
+ Hot glue and glue gun
+ 10 feet (3.04 m) of 1-inch (2.54 cm) sisal rope
+ Humility
+ A trash can (to throw it in upon completion)

STEP 1: Who Am I Really and Why?

Before you begin this project, take a minute to think about all the crappy things you've done in your life and how you probably deserve every terrible thing that has happened to

you if you really think about it. I mean, what kind of monster would try to make a fucking doorstop out of a brick and some rope? There are real people with real problems and this is what I choose to spend my time on? Take a moment right now to clench your fist and scream, "SHAME! SHAME! SHAME!" like you're at an anti-Trump rally (is he still president when this book comes out? PLEASE SAY NO OH GOD PLEASE SAY NO!).

STEP 2: Glue the Goddamn Cork Thing onto the Brick

Using a glue gun and COMMON FUCKING SENSE attach the cork doodad that you found in the gardening section of the hardware store to the bottom of the brick (cork side faces away from brick).

STEP 3: Begin the Coil of Death

By this point in the project, you'll have started asking yourself, "Should I really be doing this? It's gonna look like shit!" DON'T LET THESE INNER NEGATIVE THOUGHTS KEEP YOU FROM PERSEVERING. Just think if Columbus hadn't persevered. There'd be a whole culture of people inhabiting America, not ruining everything, living sustainably and respectfully and not destroying the land. Oh wait, bad example! Anyway, keep going or don't keep going. I've already told you this project is garbage. But if you are moving forward, cut the end of your rope at a 45-degree angle and use that

as the beginning of the coil. Use your hot glue to attach the rope to itself, asking yourself continually, "WHY AM I MAKING THIS?"

STEP 4: Attach That Glue Coil Mess on the Brick

Still not sure why I'm including this in the book? Me neither. Anyway, use a shit-ton of hot glue to affix the coil mess you just made to the top of the brick. This will hold it in place so you can coil it around the rest of the brick.

STEP 5: Keep Gluing Until You Start Questioning Reality

At this point, you're just doing this because you don't want to admit failure. Keep wrapping the rope around the brick, gluing as you go. Give yourself a little smile as you do this. A smile that says, "I got a book deal and I chose to use it to publish a story about how much of a loser I am. This is why I'll die alone." A fun fact about the photo shoot for this book is that I have a rare disease called Resting Bitch Face that causes me to scowl every time I do anything or quite frankly any time I am awake and not actively trying to smile. For this book I had to try to do little weird half smiles so I wouldn't look like I was pissed off the whole time. THESE ARE TRUE STORIES ABOUT REAL LIFE YOU GUYS. Clearly I went a little overboard with this half smile.

STEP 6: Finish the Coil ARE WE DONE YET I'M SO EMBARRASSED

Continue wrapping the rope around the brick until it reaches the bottom. At the base, make sure to use an ample amount of hot glue. While you do this, think about how incredible an invention hot glue is. Like think about the olden days, when pioneer women would struggle to make ugly rope doorstops using glue made from goat's blood (or whatever they used back then). We are lucky to be living in this time, even if we totally waste all our modern amenities by making garbage like this piece-of-shit doorstop.

STEP 7: Literally Throw It in the Garbage and Drink a Bottle of Wine by Yourself

That's what I did. This was in the middle of writing this book when I was totally overwhelmed and feeling completely crazy. This was the only DIY I hadn't done before and the only one I wasn't into at all. But I've said it before and I'll say it again and again and again until my face explodes, you gotta try shit in order to make cool shit.

A SIDE PIECE FOR YOUR SOFA

Side tables serve an important function in our society. They keep larger pieces of furniture company by acting as a mediator between their height and the floor. They also keep furniture from looking too naked and exposed. Sometimes, the sides of a sofa feel bashful if they're not partially covered by a side table. Sofas are modest people with family values, and they don't always want their completely nude bodies exposed to the entire world. They are codependent and needy, and often like to be accompanied by a side table.

It can be difficult to know when and where a side table is necessary, but you can usually do so by asking yourself a series of questions:

1. Is there room for a side table?

2. Will a side table make the room look crowded?

3. Is there a functional need for a side table (i.e., is there anywhere else one could put a cocktail if they were sitting in the seat in question)?

4. Will the side table visually enhance the room?

5. Is the side of the furniture piece in question flat or rounded (this won't determine whether you should have a side table or not, but might determine what shape it should be)?

6. Will everyone think you're poor and disgusting if you DON'T have a side table?

7. Will everyone think you're tacky and rich if you DO have a side table?

Clearly, the questions surrounding side tables are fraught with worry and doubt, and it will be years before we get to the bottom of the existential crisis that is the question, "Do I need a side table?" But here's my tip: if you think you might need a side table, you need a side table. So why not try making this supereasy/relatively cheap one

I made. Like me, this table is simple, yet elegant and goes with everything. And regaling your friends with the story of how you made it is a great conversation boost when things get awkward and/or antagonistic at a dinner party. Follow along as I take you on a journey. A journey to the new side table you've always dreamed of.

HOW TO MAKE IT!

What You'll Need:

+ **4 pieces of 2 x 12 x 24-inch (5 x 30 x 60.9 cm) pine wood**

+ **3-inch (7.6 cm) wood screws**

+ **Wood glue**

+ **Sandpaper (heavy, medium, and fine grit)**

+ **A putty knife**

+ **A drill**

+ **White semigloss paint**

+ **A paintbrush (for the paint, DUH)**

+ **A pink shirt**

Just kidding, you don't need a pink shirt for this.

STEP 1: Hire a Dude You Don't Know to Cut Some Pieces of Wood for You

As I've said in previous chapters, if you can trick someone else into doing work you can later take credit for, by all means please do so. So instead of buying long-ass planks of pine and jamming them into your car (think of the interior!), go to a hardware store or lumberyard and ask them to cut the pieces down for you. For my side table, I used 24-inch-long (60.9 cm) pieces to create a rectangular side table that is nearly a square. But you can use this idea to make a side table any size.

STEP 2: Sand the Fuck Out of Everything!

The key to this project not turning out like garbage is sanding so long and hard that by the time you're done your arms are just stumps sticking out of your torso. Smooth, beautiful stumps without even a lick of texture on them because you're worked your way from a large-grit sandpaper to a very fine-grit sandpaper. Sanding is a process and you'll def need a friend to keep you company while you do it or you'll lose your mind. Sanding is really fucking boring. And you swallow so much dust. In fact, looking back on this photo shoot I'm getting really pissed that none of you showed up to help me sand. WHERE WERE YOU WHEN I NEEDED YOU??? Try to sand out as much of the natural texture as you can, concentrating most fully on the ends of the pieces that will be exposed once the side table is assembled.

STEP 3: Predrill Holes

In order for the 3-inch (7.6 cm) wood screws I made you buy to screw in easily, you'll need to first drill a hole into the wood. The predrilled holes should be slightly smaller than the screws themselves so they have something to catch on. At this point, you should have a friend help you hold the wood pieces together. Everything is better with a friend!

STEP 4: Apply Glue

The weird thing about wood glue is that it's actual magic from real witches. It can take something that would

normally fall apart in one minute and make it strong, sturdy, handsome, and masculine, like me. Make sure to use a lot of wood glue to attach the four pieces that make up this side table. If you don't, your table will fall apart and everyone will laugh at you.

STEP 5: Screw It!

This part is relatively self-explanatory. Here, you're simply drilling the pieces together to make your side table into a square. What would be helpful here is to have another person help you hold this in place so it's not wobbling all over the table and nearly impossible to keep straight. But

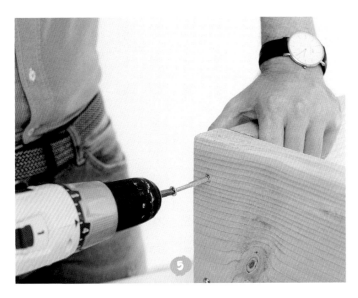

the only other person around while I was doing this was the photographer, and he was busy taking the photographs so I couldn't make him help me. Ultimately it would have been nice if someone had shown up to help me hold this wobbly-ass collection of garbage boards together while I was drilling them but I didn't have any friends so I did it alone. Was it a metaphor for my life? Yes? Would I do it again? Yes? AND SO CAN YOU!

STEP 6: Filler, It's Not Just for Faces Anymore!

If you're anything like the people I know in Los Angeles, your face and body are basically balloons filled with Rejuvaderm MD. However, through modern science, the miracle of filler has now extended into the wonderful world of wood! You too can use wood filler to fill in the gaps and cracks that are inevitable when you're an idiot who doesn't know what he's doing making things at home. Use a simple putty knife to apply a liberal amount of wood filler to any cracks or gaps and allow it to dry. Once it's dry, sand it and move on.

STEP 7: Paint, Betch!

You guys, this is literally the only fun part of this whole DIY. Painting is therapeutic and relaxing. Unless you get paint all over your pink shirt and have to run to the bathroom screaming, "I LOVE THIS SHIRT," hoping that you'll get the paint out before it sets (I got it out don't worry). Pro Tip: Don't wear cute, colorful clothes while you paint (unless you're writing a design book and are trying to act fancy in front of your readers). Because this wood is superabsorbent and you were too lazy to prime this shit, you'll need at least three coats. Opt for smooth, thin coats over chunky, thick coats.

STEP 8: ACCESSORIZE!

This type of side table is supersimple to create and can be made in any size, wide or thin, tall or short. But it can be difficult to accessorize due to its open center. For mine, I chose a stack of books, a vessel, and a decorative box. If you're looking for an eclectic look, you'll want some items that give it height and take up visual space within the cube. If the space it's going in is more minimal, you can get away with leaving it a bit more open.

MAKING A WOODEN BENCH AS SIMPLE AS YOUR MOM

Benches answer an eternal question that has plagued people all over the world since the beginning of time: "WHAT SHOULD I PUT THERE???" Scientists agree that the majority of cave paintings are basically just about cave people trying to figure out what to put in an awkward part of their house. Usually, if you're looking at a space and you have no clue what to put in it, the answer is: A BENCH.

Benches are the most versatile type of furniture in the whole entire world. They can be big or small, light or dark, wood or upholstered. They can be so big you can use them as a coffee table. Or so small you use them as a miniature dining table for photo shoots with your pet parrots. I think the reason they work so well in so many different awkward spaces is that they have a very friendly, hopeful message. A bench says, "COME SIT HERE!" And who doesn't want a place to sit!

I love an accent bench for both practical and aesthetic reasons. They can provide extra seating when you need it or a place to tie your shoes before you run out the door screaming, "I CAN'T BELIEVE I'M OVER TWO HOURS LATE TO MY OWN WEDDING!" Or they can provide a lovely place to put a nice stack of books with a decorative object up top. Benches can be trustworthy workhorses or just pretty things to look at.

Today we're going to make a bench I conceptualized while wandering the aisles of a hardware store in Palm Springs. Hardware stores are great places to get ideas, just ogling all those components and imagining what you could do with them. I tried to keep the projects in this book so simple a child could do them.

HOW TO MAKE IT!

What You'll Need:

- **2 pieces of wood, 12 x 24 x ¾ inches (30 x 60.9 x 1.9 cm)**
- **Wood glue**
- **Sandpaper (medium and fine grit)**
- **4 rectangular furniture legs**
- **4 top plates (this is the bracket that attaches your legs to the bench)**
- **Blue tape**
- **¾-inch (1.9 cm) wood screws**
- **Power drill**

STEP 1: Glue, You Simpleton!

I gotta be honest with you guys, this is one of the laziest do-it-yourself projects I've ever done. This gluing part is maybe the hardest part and it's literally gluing two pieces of wood together. I'm sorry you had to come here for

this. I'm so embarrassed. I will say that I love the way this bench turns out but it's so easy it's like you shouldn't even take credit for it. A long time ago, when women wore bonnets and men drove them around in canvas-covered wagons (before they all got superhungry and ate each other) DIYs used to be hard. But now there's the Internet and everything is easy and that's how we got to this point where I'm basically like, HEY GO TO THE STORE AND BUY SOME STUFF AND PUT IT TOGETHER THEN SAY YOU MADE IT. Whatever, it's fine. So yeah, anyway, this step is just squeezing glue all over one of the boards while yelling things about inequality. CAN YOU HANDLE IT?

STEP 2: Smash the Boards Together

For this project, I chose two slightly different tones of wood for each piece so that when you looked at them from the side there would be a color blocking situation going on. This part of the project is the most fun. You just smash those boards together while thinking about feelings you have deep inside you that you'd like to smash even deeper

inside you. It's supercute. I know I look superpeaceful in this pic, but I'm literally raging about something that's supersecret (getting dumped and laid off within two months WHILE I WAS WRITING THIS FUCKING BOOK).

STEP 3: Tape the Boards Together

To make sure the bond between these boards is as strong as the bond between Goldie Hawn and Kurt Russell, it's best to tape them together with blue tape while they dry. An added bonus of using two wood types to make this bench is that the combination of the glue and the double layered wood makes it superstrong. Just try to karate chop this in half! Make sure you tape in both directions so the bond between the boards is as strong as my devotion to you.

STEP 4: Attach the Brackets or Whatever These Things Are Called

Remember when I had braces and the most exciting part of my whole life was deciding what color rubber bands to get? That's right. I'm an eight-hundred-year-old leather woman and I got braces before Invisalign. We used to get to choose a color for the rubber bands that held the braces in place and it was literally the only joy in my life. The rubber bands were my version of an old midwestern lady sweater. Like you know how midwestern ladies wear a sweater with a Christmas tree at Christmas? I'd get red and green rubber bands at Christmas because CHRISTMAS, DUH! Anyway, this part of the project is kind of like that except not at all. You use your human arms to attach the brackets to the base of your bench seat (this is what the legs will screw into later). You do this by placing the brackets a half inch (1.27 cm) from the outside of the bench seat, predrilling holes, and then affixing the brackets with wood screws.

STEP 5: Screw in the Legs OH MY GOD IS THIS REALLY HAPPENING

You guys, I told you this was easy. This step is literally just screwing these legs you bought at the store into the bracket you just attached to the bench. This is literally the easiest thing a human has done ever.

STEP 6: More Sanding

Sanding is boring, but it's the only part of this whole project that makes it even remotely work. Stop complaining and SAND UNTIL THESE EDGES ARE SMOOTH AND ALIGNED.

STEP 7: You're Done!

Just kidding, there's not another step. This dumb DIY was so simple it doesn't require a final step!

LIFE IS MEANINGLESS LET'S MAKE A SWING SHELF

Have you ever been like, "I want to put a shelf there, but I also want to put a swing there too"? Or have you ever been like, "When I was little I asked Mama for a rope swing and she told me a rope swing was why Daddy left so we never spoke of it again?" I mean, I've literally said both those things and that's why I love anything rope-swing themed. That and the fact that a rope swing accessory brings in multiple materials and takes your space from ECK to ECLECTIC in a matter of seconds.

The thing that's fun about a swinging shelf is that it's both playful and practical. They scream, "HEY I'M A TOY," but also, "HEY YOU CAN PUT SHIT ON ME AND I'LL BE COOL WITH IT, GIRL."

HOW TO MAKE IT!

What You'll Need:

+ 8 x 24 x ¾-inch (20.3 x 60.9 x 1.9 cm) wood plank (I used poplar)

+ 4 yards of ⅜-inch (.95 cm) sisal rope

+ Brass wall-hanging hooks

+ A drill with a ⅜-inch (.95 cm) drill bit

STEP 1: Drill Some Big-Ass Holes!

The first step is to take this giant drill bit and drill some giant holes that your rope can fit through. I used a ⅜-inch (.95 cm) drill bit. It can be difficult to drill through hardwood with such a thick drill bit, so you might want to start with a smaller drill bit and work your way up.

STEP 2: Cut the Cord!

Using scissors, cut the rope to the length you want your shelf to hang at. I chose a 16-inch (40.6 cm) hang altogether, which meant that I doubled the 16 inches (40.6

cm) and added 4 inches (10.16 cm, for the space between the holes). Altogether it was 36 inches (91.4 cm). You can hang your shelves at whatever height you want because this is a free country and YOU ARE SPECIAL.

STEP 3: Thread the Rope!

It's probably physically possible to thread the rope through the small holes you created, but I wouldn't recommend it. I wrapped the ends in blue painter's tape to make it easier to thread through. It's a scientific fact that all designers love blue tape, so I try to use it in every project I do!

STEP 4: Pull the Rope!

At this step, you'll need to decide how low you want your shelf to hang. This will be determined by the space you're putting it in and how much clearance there is. I chose a 16-inch (40.6 cm) drop from the top of the rope to the shelf. To make sure that the shelf hangs evenly, measure and mark at 16 inches (40.6 cm or whatever height you choose), making sure you're keeping the lower rope flush with the table.

STEP 5: Loop It Up!

This is where things get crazy. You're going to create a loop using glue. Make sure to use a liberal amount of glue so the whole thing is strong and secure.

STEP 6: Wrap It with Wire and Cut the Excess Rope

One thing I learned as a boy growing up in the forest is that you can use wire for just about anything. My sister and I used to make Barbie clothes out of wire. I made a lamp out of wire. Wire is literally a miracle material. So it came as no surprise to me that I figured out a way to incorporate wire into this project. The wire will hold the rope together while it dries, the glue will keep it strongly bound for years and years and years.

STEP 7: Hide Your Sins

Wire is a miracle material, but its look doesn't necessarily mesh with the aesthetic of this project. We're going to use some smaller rope to cover it, giving the whole thing a warm, beachy vibe. Start by tying one end of a piece of thin rope around the end of the wired area, wrapping your way around until all the wire is covered. Tie off and cut the excess rope.

STEP 8: Hang That Shit!

For the final step, you're going to need to measure the width between the two sets of holes you created on either side of your shelf. Then you'll need to install hooks at the same width 16 inches (40.6 cm or whatever height you chose) above where you want the shelf to be.

WHY DESIGN MATTERS

As you may have noticed from reading this book, I think a lot about everything all the time and it's annoying. One of the things I think about is why design matters. Part of me always sort of wrote it off it as a superficial, surface-oriented endeavor. Which it is to a certain degree. But it's also an art form, a way of expressing who you are and how you want to live your life. Interior design is mostly about sitting with yourself and asking questions like, What is important to me? How do I see myself? And how do I want to live my life? Or WHAT THE FUCK LAMP SHOULD I CHOOSE?

These aren't unimportant questions. They are at the very core of our human existence (sidenote: THIS JUST GOT SO DRAMATIC). Making decisions about what to put in your house requires that you put your thinking cap on and try to imagine what you will be doing in the space. Will you be sitting a lot? Or will you be standing, awkwardly? Will there be a lot of guests coming over? Or will it mostly just be you, pacing, wondering where your life went wrong? You're literally creating the canvas upon which your life happens.

Interior design isn't just about practicality and function. It's also about creating a space which makes you feel that you're living your best life. A good example is a piece of accent furniture you know you'll never use. Say a bench in your bedroom that you know you'll never sit on. Why is it there? It's there because every time you see it, it tells your subconscious, "Hey, Subconscious, you could sit here if you want! It's comfy and cozy and supportive up in here!" It's about reassurance, showing yourself you have a nice life. Sometimes seeing (cute furniture in your house) is believing.

Interior design is as much about creating spaces that are beautiful, comfortable, and elegant as it is about creating spaces that speak to your dreams and desires. Creating a nice space tells yourself, "Yay! I'm going to have a nice life here!" Creating a nice space for someone else shows them, "Hey, I care about you! I would def help you put on your oxygen mask in a plane crash (after I've put mine on as per FAA regulations duh!) and I want to make a nice space for you so you have a nice life." Interior design is a way of showing care for yourself and care for other people.

DESIGN CAN MAKE YOU A BETTER PERSON

Can design change your life, make you successful, get you a husband, and make you rich? HELLO YES DUH WERE YOU PAYING ATTENTION THE LAST 230 PAGES!?! The whole point of design is tricking others (and yourself) into thinking you're less garbage-y than you actually are. And all that stuff I said above about creating a beautiful space where your beautiful life can take place. Just like dressing nicely can change your day and make you feel like a more confident, attractive, and capable person, creating a beautiful home quietly tells yourself, "Hey, Self, you're the shit and you deserve this!"

NOW IT'S TIME TO YELL AT OTHER PEOPLE

Did you like what I had to say in here? Now it's your turn. Go to a friend's house and immediately scream, "THIS RUG IS HIDEOUS LET ME BUY YOU A NEW ONE!" or "DID THAT DISGUSTING CHANDELIER COME WITH THE HOUSE?" Telling people subtly that you hate their homes is a small way you can help them live their best lives.

Just kidding, that's a bad strategy. But what you *can* do is run around like a crazy person talking about decor and home furnishing ideas you love. Get them thinking about design. Take them to stores. This is the way to get people with ugly-ass houses to have houses that are less ugly-ass. And it's a way you can literally help them have a better life.

YOU GUYS YOU DID IT!

You made it through my book! Through the ups, the downs, that one time I made a superugly doorstop that I should have just edited out of the book but kept in because I thought it was funny that I'm such a huge fuckup. It's been a really great journey, right? You learned all sorts of stuff you wanted to learn about design, DIY, and life. But mostly you learned a bunch of nonsense about my personal life I had no real reason for telling you aside from the fact that I have way too many feelings and not enough space in my body to contain them.

Here's what I'll leave you with. I hope in all my joking around, oversharing, and transparency about my mistakes, I've shown you that the most important part of creating a beautiful life for yourself is to be fearless, not ashamed of your lack of expertise, not to hide when you go through something difficult. My goal with everything I do is to inspire people, people with a fuck-ton of money and people like me who are basically broke, to do whatever they can to show pride in their personal space.

Showing yourself that you matter by making your space as beautiful as possible is a way to improve your life. For rich-ass people, this might be a little easier because they can just hire someone like me to come over and throw pillows all over the place until it looks gorgeous. For normal-ass people like you and me, resourcefulness is key. We gotta be creative. Which is why I included DIY as part of this book. If you can't afford to buy that fancy one, figure out a way to make it yourself. Or find a vintage one. Whatever you do, NEVER GIVE UP! You're literally worth it.

Whether it be choosing decor for your home, making your own dumb tray, or figuring out how to navigate living with a roommate, you can do it! You innately know the answers to all of life's challenges, you just normally wait until you read them in a book to trust that you know what you're doing. Let's be honest, I have no idea what I'm doing. And you just listened to me blab for a whole goddamn book. THE ANSWERS ALREADY LIE WITHIN YOU.

So go fix your house, go make some stuff, go deal with all the bullshitty bullshit life throws your way. I command thee.

GET IT TOGETHER!

ACKNOWLEDGMENTS

This book is really dedicated to my parents but I wanted to make that stupid joke about not having a boyfriend on the dedication page so I'm writing that here. I guess that shows you what a shitty son I am. CATHERINE, you took me everywhere, exposed me to the most incredible art, performance, and life experiences out there. I am a creative person because of you. DALE, you always expected the best of me and knew I could do it. I owe my ambition and education to your belief in me. Oh, just FYI Catherine and Dale are my parents. I grew up calling them by their first names. DEAL WITH IT!

It goes without saying that this book is the result of collaborations with numerous people and that it would just look like the scribblings of a deranged bag lady without all their help. The most important of these collaborators is ZEKE RUELAS, the incredible photographer who shot all these beautiful images. It's hard to know unless you've worked on photo shoots how much labor, planning, and production goes into creating just one stupid image. Each of the images in this book took an average of three hours to compose (some much less, some more). I didn't have any help on these shoots so Zeke was tasked not only with shooting these images, but with helping me move giant furniture pieces around, move disgustingly heavy bags of props from my car, and even assisting in finishing DIY projects as we raced against the rapidly approaching sunset. I am so proud of the gorgeous images in this book and it's obvious to anyone who sees them that it would be complete garbage without them.

AMY SLY, the revoltingly talented book designer took the mishmash of insanity that I sent, with an incredibly complex system of images, text callbacks, illustrations, and not-alway-easy-to-place rants, and created a logical system that made it so much easier to say what I wanted to say, give the tips I wanted to give, and write the jokes I wanted to write.

HOLLY LA DUE, my editor, had to keep this book on track (and keep me productive) as my life took a nosedive into the dumpster (I was laid off and dumped simultaneously, did you catch that?). It can be hard to keep creatives on task, especially when they hate their lives and would rather be lying in bed wondering why life sucks so much. Holly basically had to call me every day and tell me to do everything like a thousand times before I actually did it. That must have been superannoying. Thanks, Holly!

Thank you to the homeowners who generously let me use their homes as shooting locations: CARRIE and JOHN QUINTANAR, MATTHEW LANPHIER, JASON MICALLEF, DONNIE and RYAN DIXON-HADEN, PATRICK POCKLINGTON, ERIKA and JASON DOBKIN, JARED PETER, and JIM HANSEN. The stories that I related to the images of their homes have literally nothing to do with the homeowners so don't judge them, OK?

Thanks to KELLY OXFORD and JEFFERY SELF for vetting some of my joke ideas. And thanks to my siblings ELISA and MIGUEL. They did literally nothing to help me with this book but I feel obligated to thank them because we're related.

OK bye.

INDEX

Page references in *italics* refer to photographs.

A

accents, decorative, 27, 42, 59
  benches as, 224, *225*, 232
  brass, 19
  contemporary, 19, 24, 52, 59–60
  eclectic, 24, 67, 88, 211, 223
  formal, 41, 42, 44, 45,
  fun, 15, 79, 229
  global, 71
  industrial, 126
  oversize stuffed animals as, *117*, 120
  round tables as, 45
  rugs as, 91
  structural, 24
  unexpected, 42
accessories, 34, 60, 71, 223
  collecting 60, 114
  hate of, 128
  on kitchen countertops, 144, *145*, 159
  on shelves, 35, 36, 60, 176
  reflect your personality, 114
  sports-related, *121*, 128
  striped, 44
  tabletop, 138, 159
  vary size of, 35
  vintage, 25, 95
  with faces, *85*, *105*, *112*, 113, 114
aesthetics
  and design solutions, 100, 224
  angled, 60
  Japanese, 113
  of Spanish tile, 52
alcohol, 186
  at parties, 138–40
  cocktails, 131, 138, 139, 140, 220
  wine, 140, 147, 148, 186, 199
alcoholism, 139, 186
Andy Warhol Diaries, 9, 48
apartments, 56, 58–59, 67, 77, 85, 122,
    144, 171, 182, 216
  in Los Angeles, 46, 63, 65
  in New York, 46, 124, 191
  in Santa Cruz, 119
  revenge, 105
Apple Doll
  face, 15
  Lady, 29
apron-awnings, 24
arches
  on doors, *47*, 50, *50*, *53*
  on windows, 50, *50*

architectural details, 25, 50, 59, 60
art; artwork, 67, 71, 111, 128
  affording, 35, 96
  circular, 27, *28*
  creating, 107
  framing, 99, *99*
  gallery walls, *52*, 67, *69*, 82, 85–87, *87*,
    156
    rivers (spaces between art), 86
  hanging, 82–87
  large-scale, *66*, 67, *71*
  lighter-weight, 85
  one-of-a-kind, 35
  on shelves, 36
  vintage, 96, 99
  wall paper framed, as, *33*, 35
artists, 68, 71, 96, 133, 188
art school, 77
Austra (band), 185

B

babies, 79, 174–77
  gifts for, 177
baby boomer, 111
baby showers, 194
balance, achieving, 19, 36, 88, 95, 123
ball gowns, 19, 41
Barcelona, 24
bars, home, 128, *128*
baseboards, 60
bathrooms, 60, 79, 154
  statement, 25
bathtubs, 67, 215
  hanging light fixtures above, 101
Baughman, Milo, 128
beach
  house, 31–37
  -inspired children's room, 121, *121*
bedrooms, 19, 42, *42*, 60, 67, 232
  children's, 48, 49, *116*, 117, *117*, *118*,
    119, *119*, 120–21, *121*
  color in, 60, 67, 79, 107, 119, 121
  faces in, *112*, 113
  guest, 25, 108, *108*, 113, *113*, 141, 156
  master, 27, 42, *42*, 60
beds
  art above, 35
  custom-designed, 62
  eating in, *170*, 173
  gold pillows on, *64*, 67
  light fixtures over, 101

parent's, 174
placement of, 102
seating at end of, 42, *42*, 232
twin, 156
upholstered, 42, *42*, 60
with brass accents, *16–17*, 19
benches, wooden, how to make, 224,
    224–25, 226–27, *226–27*
Benjamin Moore paint colors
  Half Moon Crest, 77
  Horizon, 77
  Sleigh Bells, 76, *76*, 77
  Super White, 77
big-box stores, 36, 63, 148, 206
bins, storage, 121
Björk swan dress, 114, 194
Black Crow Studios, wallpaper from, 35
blaming, 111, 179, 191–92
bookcases, 96, 121, 176
books
  advice, 182, 186
  diet, 181
  on benches, 224, *225*
  on coffee tables, *52*, *69*, 207, *207*, 208,
    210
  on dressers, *81*, 96, *96*, *119*
  on shelves, 35, 36, *36–37*
  on side tables, *65*, *221*, 223, *225*
  on trays, *52*, 211
borders, 25
boyfriends, 62, 122, 170–73. *See also*
    friends
  ex-, 56, 67, 99, 107, 155, 165, 173, 182
  imaginary 5, 11, 56
  moving in with, 56, 58–59
  sofas as, 107
  youthful, 14
brass, 19
  brackets, 208
  hangers, 83, 229
breakups, 62, 104–5, 182–87
bros, 122, 123, 124, 126, 128
budgets, limited, 35, 65, 68, 95, 147
built-ins, 35, 44, *44*

C

candelabra, *51*
  wooden bird, *58*, *94*, 96
candles
  in guest room, 156, *156*
  on coffee tables, 210

with faces, *112*, 113
Cape Cod style, 42, 48
carafes for water, 144, *144*, *173*
cat face, 14, 15, 22
chairs, 13
    arranging, 67, 138
    vintage, 19
challenges, 10, 182, 191, 233
champagne, 154, *154*
chandeliers
    above dining room tables, *20*, *60–61*,
        101, *101*, *203*
    hanging, 101, *101*
    in bedrooms, 101
    in hallways, *89*, 101
    in kitchens, 101
    in living rooms, 101
    Orblandos (wired chandeliers), 202, *203*,
        204–5, *204–5*
character, adding, 19, 60, 67, 95
children; kids, 29, 48–49, 196, 197
    babies, 174–77
    bedrooms, 49, 115–21, *116*, *117*, *118*,
        119, *120*, *121*
    toys, 46, 121
"chill," 56, 123
cleaning house, 138, 151, 152, 158–59,
    161, 171, 208
cloths, cleaning, reusable, *109*, *158*, 159
clutter, 27, 128
coastal hints, *30*, 34, *34*
coasters, 138
cocktail, 139, 140, 220
    dispensers, 144
    garnishes, 139
    glasses, 140
    parties, 131, 138, 139, 144
    sparkling spiked lemonade, 139
    tequila limeade, 139
coffee, 151, 180, 206
coffee-making paraphernalia, 39, 56, 144
coffee tables, *19*, *32*, *40*, *51*, *52*, *57*, 67,
    91, 99, *106–7*, 158, 159, *209*, 215, 224
    books, 207
    contemporary, 59
    farm style, 41, 44
    flowers on, *19*, *36*, *39*, *44*, *105*, *106*, *124*,
        207, *207*
    how to make, 208–10, *208–10*
    mid-century, 128
    rules for placement, 209
collections, 114
    art, 56, 96
    colored glass, 53, *53*
    dishes; platters, 143, 148
    spices, 144, *145*
    spoons, 39
    tchotchkes, 60
color, 15, 36, 67, 74, 126
    accents, 45, 60, 79, 90, 132

color blocking, 121, 226
colors, 15, 42, 60, 74, 77, 132
    beige, 19, 35, 77
    blue, 25, 34, 45, 60, 67, 74, 126
    classic, 45, 77
    darker, 42
    desaturated, 77
    fun, 74, 75, 79, 121
    gray, 62, 74, 77, 101
    green, 44, 45
    Half Moon Crest, 77
    Horizon, 77
    lighter, 74
    navy blue, 45, 60
    neutral, 74, 77
    pink, 19, 107
    preppy, 35, 45
    sandy, 34, 35
    saturated, *40–41*, 42, 44, 74, *78*, 90, 119
    Sleigh Bells, *76*, *76*, 77
    Super White, 77
    wall, 59, 67, 74–77, 79–80
    white, 25, 45, 53, 60, 74, 75, 101
color test sheet, 77
color wheel, 74, 77, *77*
comfortable spaces, creating, 42, 48, 49,
    65, 88, 91, 108, 232
concerts, going to, 185
container gardens, 162, *163*, *164*, 165–67,
    166, *167*
contemporary
    accents, 19, 24, 52, 59–60
    definition, 59
    furnishings, 19
    homes, 24, 25, 59, 60, 74
    light fixtures, 52
control over things and events, 10, 122,
    191
conversation circle, 67
cooking
    at home, 25, 45, 48, 108, 144, 147, 152
    spices, 144, *145*
crafting skills, 9, 10, 188, 201, 206, 211
Craftsmen style, 48
creativity, 65
crocodile stool, 42, *42*
CrossFit, 15, 82
crow's feet, 15
cultural appropriation, age of, 71
curtains, hanging too high, 103, *103*. *See
    also* drapery

D
death, 67, 101, 171, 177, 182, 187, 191
decals, 121
dens, 44
depression, 10–11, 68, 182, 185, 186, 187
despair, 186
diagonal, placing furniture on, 102, *102*
diary, reading your roommate's, *172*, 173

Didion, Joan, 55
diets, 140, 178, 179, 181. *See also* food
    Orlandiet, 180–81
dining rooms, *20*, *24*, *25*, 60–61, 67, 79, 90
dining tables, 15, *20*, *24*, 60–61, 224
    flowers on, *2*, *20*, 60, *149*, 151, *151*,
        161, *203*
    light fixtures over, *20*, 60–61, 101, *101*,
        129, 202, *203*
    settings on, *2*, 60–61, *149*, 151, *151*, 159
dinner, 140
    appropriate behavior at, 173
    parties, 15, 144, 146–48, 151, 220
    potluck, 147–48
    texting at, 173
dishes. *See also* plates
    cleaning, 151, 171
    colorful, 53, 143
    reusable, 140, 148
    serving platters, *146*, 148, *151*
    white, *2*, *60–61*, *142*, 143, *143*, 148, *149*,
        151, *151*, *161*, *212*
disposable
    chopsticks, 167
    cutlery, 148
    floor cleaning pads, 159
    towels, 148, 159, 213
diversity, 90, 198
    of finishes, 19
    of materials, 25
    of shapes, 15
dogs, small, 15
Do It Yourself (DIY) projects, 10
    bench, 224, *224–25*, 226–27, *226–27*
    coffee table, 206–10, *207–10*
    doorstop, rope, 216, *217*, 218–19,
        218–19, 233
    Orblando (wire chandelier), 202, *203*,
        204–5, *204–5*
    side table, 220, *221*, 222–23, *222–23*
    succulent container garden, 162, *163*,
        164, 165–67, *166*, *167*
    swing shelf, *228*, 229–31, *229–31*
    tray, 211, *212*, 213–15, *213–15*
doors; doorways, 59, 60, 75, *75*
    arched, *47*, 50, *50*, 53
    frames, 25
    open-, 156
    sliding screen, 71
doorstops, rope, 216, *217*, 218–19,
    218–19, 233
dorms, 63
drapery; drapes, 15, *20*, 42
    cleaning, 90
    custom, 41
    hanging, 82, 103, *103*
    stripes on, 41, 44
drapery rods, 103
dream home, 11, 33, 55, 100
dreams; aspirations, 22, 31, 48, 232

dressers, *81*, 91, 96, *96*, *98*, 99, *113*, *119*
drink dispensers, *137*, 138, 139, *139*, 144
    carafes for water, 144, *144*, *173*
dude design, 122, 125, 126, 128

E

eclecticism, 24, 67, 88, 211, 223, 229
elegance; elegant, 44, 60, 74, 96, 114,
    148, 220, 232
endorphins, 179
energy balance, 19
entitlement, 103, 190
entryways, 45, *47*, 50, *157*, *217*. *See also*
    foyer
Erna's Elderberry House, 115
exercise, 179, 180, 181
    CrossFit, 15, 82
    painting as, 80
experimentation, 67, 68, 100, 198, 216

F

faces, 113
    Apple Doll   face, 15
    cat face, 14, 15, 22
    gay lady, 123
    on pillows, *105*, *112*, 113
    RBF (Resting Bitch Face), 162, 195, 219
failures, 50, 68, 83, 187, 192, 216
fair trade, 71
family, 41, 45, 71, 111, 185, 190, 196
    homes, 48–49
    of friends, 185
    photographs, 113, 114, *114*, 210
    rooms, 44, 53
fat shaming, 179
faux
    finishing, 95
    -pas, 59, 101
fear; fears, 41, 46, 82, 110, 192
    of clutter, 128
    of color, 74
    of failure, 68, 216
fearless, 233
feeling
    in control, 122
    of purpose, 192
feelings, 182, 226
    expressing, 185, 187, 192
    MASC, 124
    sharing, 110, 185, 187
    too many, 56, 116, 175, 183, 233
finishes, 19, 34, 79, 108
    brass, 19
    eggshell, 79
    faux, 95
    flat, 77, 79
    gloss, 59, 77, 79
    matte, 79
    on floors, 25
    on walls, 77–79
    satin, 79

flea markets, 35, 67, 71, 95, 96, 99. *See*
    also thrift shops
    Rose Bowl Flea Market, 25
flooring; floors, 20, *20*, 25, 74, 88, 103,
    220
    with multi-colored tile pattern, 20, *20*
    wood, 88, 91
flower
    vases, 67, 132, 133–34, *134*, 207
flowers, *43*, 45, 132
    arranging, 132, 133, *133*, 134, 151
    in guest rooms, 156, *156*
    on coffee tables, *19*, *36*, *39*, *44*, *105*,
    106, *124*, 207, *207*
    on dining tables, *2*, *20*, *61*, *149*, 151,
    151, *161*, *203*
food, 135, 140, 143, 147, 148, 152, 180.
    See also diets
    fights, 108
    industry, 144
    ingredients, 180–81
    pantry, 50
    processed, 181
    processors, 39
    spices, 144
formality, 41, 42, 44, 45
formal sitting area, 44
foundational elements, 44, 99
foyer, 79. *See also* entryways
framing art, 35, 99, *99*
friends, 108, 114, 162, 179, 182, 185, 188,
    191, 192, 196–99. *See also* boyfriends
    as family, 186
    at parties, 138, 140–41, 146–48
    childhood, 46, 196–97
    gay guy, 194
    judgmental, 38–39, 41
    lack of, 10, 63
    with children, 29, 48–49, 174–77
friendship, 148, 197, 198
furniture, 88, 90, 91, 119–20, 138, 220. *See*
    also beds; benches; chairs; dressers;
    media consoles; sofas; tables
    accent, 232
    aged, 19
    buying, 10, 68
    in guest rooms, 156
    mid-century, 126
    modern, 59
    painting, 119
    placement of, 207
    preppy, 42
    vintage, 19, 48, 95

G

gallery walls, *52*, 67, *69*, 73, 82, 85–87, *86*
    in bedrooms, *87*, 156
    rivers (spaces between art), 86
gardening, 162, *163*, *164*, 165–67, *166*,
    167
Gay; gays, 14, 123, 179, 185

Aged, 19
bros, 123
coming-out story, 122
Fashion Gays, 14
grief, 186
guy friends, 194
internet dating sites, 123
lady faces, 123
MASC4MASC, 123
Men in Palm Springs, 166
middle age, 14
signs of aging, 14–15
weddings, 194
wellbeing, 20
Youth slang, 15
gender
    as a construct, 122
    identity, 124, 126
Generation X, 111
generosity, 198
glasses; glassware, *137*, 138, 140, *140*,
    148, *149*, *151*, *161*, *173*, 206, 215
global
    style, 71
    warming, 34, 154
glow
    balloons, 141
    sticks, 141, 198
glue, 231
    gun, 216, 218, *218*, *219*
    hot, 216, 218, 219
    wood, 211, 213, *213*, 214, 220, 222,
    222, 224, *224*, 226
Goula / Figuera, 24
graffiti, 128
guest rooms, 25, 35, 48, 108, 113, *113*,
    141
    candles in, 156, *156*
    flowers in, 156, *156*
    furniture in, 156
guests, 15, 38
    at parties, 136, 138, 139, 141, 147, 151
    hosting, 131, 152, 154–56
    notes for, 154, 155, *155*
    pleading with, 67
    seating for, 55, 108, 138
    snacks for, 155, *155*
    toothbrushes for, 154, *154*
    unwanted, 152, 154, 155, 56

H

hallways
    display photographs in, 113, 114
    hanging light fixtures in, *88*, 101
    rugs in, *89*, 90
hand-dyed textiles, 53
hanging art, 35, 73, 82–87
    tools needed, 83, 85, *85*
    hanging height, 82–83, 84
hardware stores, 77, 211, 213, 216, 218,
    222, 224

hay bales as seating at a wedding, 55
heartache, 187
height, decorative, 27, 223
Henderson, Emily, 11, 191, 202
    Design Star, 191
    Emily Henderson Design, 46
HGTV, 188, 192
historic
    presence, 19, 27, 35, 95
    style, 52–53
hobbies, 27, 181. *See also* gardening
Hollywood, 22
    apartments, 63, 65
    parties, 29
    sets, food on, 180
Hollywood Hills, 25, 65
honesty, 181, 187, 192
hostess gifts, 154
hosting parties, 48, 135–36, 138–41, 146,
    148, 151
housekeepers, 138, 158, 171
humor as coping mechanism, 185

I

"influencers," 103, 187, 216
instincts, 96, 117
interior design
    fundamentals, 13–71, 80
    importance, 10, 73, 188, 232
    rules, 11, 36, 83, 90, 101, 114, 207
introducing yourself at parties, 29

J

Japanese
    aesthetic, 71, 113
    screens, 64, 67
jobs, 22, 31, 46, 100, 103, 188, 191, 192
    finding, 188, 191, 192
    layoffs as opportunities, 191, 192
    loss of, 11, 182, 187, 190, 192
judging goggles, 38, 39

K

kitchen
    accessories, 144
    canisters, *142*, 144
    counters, 39, 41, *53*, *109*, *142*, *143*,
        144, *145*
    cupboards, *53*, 144
    necessities, 143–44, *143–45*, 148, 151
    rugs, 90
kitchens, 25, 79, 108, *109*, *142*, 143–45
    cleaning, 151, 171
    congregating in, 138
    hanging light fixtures in, 101
    open, 45, *45*
    paint finish for, 79
Kondo, Marie, 59

L

Lanphier, Matthew, 20, 234
late arrivals, 29
laughter, 10, 11, 14
layering
    place settings, 151
    rugs, 91
leather, 25, 128
    sofas, *23*, *26–27*, 52, *52*, *125*
Leibovitz, Annie, 114
libraries, 35, 79
light, 67, 143
    natural, 25, 42, 44, 74
    protection, 20
light fixtures, 24, 74. *See also* chandeliers;
        Orblandos
    ceiling, 60
    contemporary, 52
    modern, 25
    sculptural, 24
    traditional, 52
    wrought iron, *51*, 52
linen
    sheets, 128, 173
    table linens, 148, 159
living rooms, *32–33*, 34, 107
    coffee tables in, *19*, *32*, *39*, *40*, *44*, *52*,
        57, *91*, *106–7*, 206, *206*, 207, *207*
    comfortable seating in, 108
    paint finishes in, 79
    photographs in, *111*, 113, 114, *114*
    rugs in, 90, *90*, 91, *91*
    televisions in, 44, *44*
Los Angeles (L.A.), 22, 140, 188, 190. *See
        also* Hollywood; Hollywood Hills
    Angelenos, 22, 24
    apartments, 46, 63, 65
Los Angeles Design Group, 24
loyalty, 197, 198
lumber yards, 222

M

maids, 158
male gender identity, 124
man cave, 123
MASC culture, 122, 123, 124, 126, 128
MASC4MASC, 123, 124, 128
masculine design, 122
masculinity, 107, 122, 124, 128
media consoles, 44, 91, *126*
mediums, distribution of, in gallery walls,
    86
menu, go-to, 148
metabolism, 165, 179
Meyers, Nancy, 45
mid-century
    furniture, 126, 128
    styles, 24, 120
midlife crisis, 14–15
Millennials, 110, 111, 114

mineral oil, 215
minimal design, 71, 124
minimalism, 24, 62, 124
minimal spaces, 27, 59, 60, 124, 223
mirrors, round, 25, *51*, *90*, *99*, *106*
mistakes, 9, 11, 46, 87, 90, 91, 100–102
    blaming others for, 192
    DIY, 216
    laughing at others', 10
    linguistic, 56
mixing
    accessories, 114
    cocktails, 139, 140
    eras of furniture, 19
    flower varieties, 133
    formal and informal, 41, 48
    friends, 199
    materials, 25, 67, 99
    paints, 77
    scale, 86
    shapes, 15
    styles, 52, 67, 86
    vintage and new, 48, 95
modern, 59, 60
    lighting, 25
    minimalism, 124
    spaces, 25, 74
moldings, 25, 59, 74. *See also* trims
    crown, 60
    rectangular, 59
mops, reusable, *158*, 159
moving in together, 56, 58–59
multi-functional space, 25
music, 14, 15, 185
music room, *52*, 95

N

napkins, 148
neighbors, one-up your, 41
networking, 29, 192
New York, 9, 48, 68, 104, 191
    apartments, 46, 65
nihilism, 186
nursery, 79
nutrition, 179–81

O

Orblandos (wire chandeliers), 202, *203*,
    204–5, *204–5*
order in the world, 122
organizing, 68
    children's rooms, *119*, 120, *120*, 121
    conversation circles, 67
    kitchens, 144
    parties, 138
    shelf-scapes, 211

P

painter's tape, blue, 85, *85*, 121, 185, 226,
    226, 230, *230*

painting
    furniture gold, 119
    pajamas, 138
    rooms, 44, 74, 80, 101, 121, 223
    tables, 223, *223*
    trays, 215, *215*
paintings, 25, 27, 35, 67, 99, 224
palate cleanser, 42
Palm Springs, 22, 166, 224
Paltrow, Gwyneth, 38, 41, 152
pantry, 50, 53, *53*
paper
    napkins, 148
    plates, 148
    towels, 148, 159, 213
parties, 25, *135*, 136, *141*, 199
    bachelor(ette), 194
    Christmas, 48
    clean up after, 151
    cocktail, 131, 138, 139, 144
    costumes, 138
    dinner, 15, 144, 146–51
    favors, 141
    Hollywood, 29
    invite list, 136
    music at, 15
    organizing, 138
    Oscar, 108
    pumpkin-carving, 216
    re-arranging space for, 138
    start time, 140
    toys, 141, *141*
patterns, 20
    multi-colored tile, 20, *20*
    trellis, *50–51, 52, 53, 64*
    wave, 121, *121*
perfection, 41, 46, 48, 49, 50, 100, 187, 192
personality, 67, 96, 111, 113
    home reflects your, 48–49, 110–11, 113–14
photograph albums, 114
photographs
    black-and-white horse, 126
    displaying, 59, *97*, 111, *111*, 113, 114, *114*, 210
pillows, 15, 53
    with faces, *105, 112*, 113
placemats, *2, 149*, 151, *151. 161*
place settings, *2*, 148, *149*, 151, *151, 161*
planks, wooden, for serving cheese, *130*, 148
plastic
    -cancer, 154
    cups, 148
    surgery, 14, 24, 88
    vacuum cleaners, 159
plates, 143, 148. *See also* dishes
platters, serving, 148, *151*
pottery, 175, 176

preppy
    colors, 45
    furnishings, 42
    nautical stripes, 35
privacy, 20
privilege, 191
    male, 124
    thin, 179

R
rage, 49, 62, 107, 162, 165, 167, 174, 211
    diva, 177
rager, 135
refrigerators, 139, 152, *152*, 162
rejection, 104, 190
relationships, 62, 182, 186
resourcefulness, 65, 67, 68, 233
resources, limited, 65, 67
restaurants, 115, 147, 148
restoring items, 96, 99
revenge, 105, 186
roommates, 170–73, 233
rope
    doorstops, 216, *217*, 218–19, *218–19*, 233
    swing shelf, *228*, 229–31, *229–31*
Rose Bowl Flea Market, 25
rug pads, 82
rugs, 42, 67, 121
    as sound buffers, 88
    cleaning, 90
    colors of, 90
    high-pile, 88
    in hallways, *89*, 90
    in kitchens, 90
    kilim, 90
    moving, 82
    rectangular, 90, *90*, 91
    round, 90, *90*, 91
    runner, 90
    selecting, 88, *89*–91, 202
    sisal, 34, 128
    size, 90, *90*, 91
    trellis-patterned, *50–51, 52, 53, 64*
    vintage, 90
rules, design
    absence of, 36
    exceptions to, 11, 74, 102, 114
    for coffee tables, 207
    for hanging art, 83, 84
    for hanging light fixtures, 52, 101
    for placing and selecting furniture, 68, 102
    for selecting colors, 60, 74, 77
    for styling shelves, 36

S
sanding, 213, *213*, 222, *222*, 223, 227
scale, 36
    mixture of, 86

of art, 36, 86
of rugs, 90
of vases, 134
scarves, 15
screens, Japanese, *64*, 67
sculptural elements, 15
Self, Jeffery, 173, 234
self-acceptance, 100, 179, 181
self-awareness, 181
self-confidence, 181, 188, 199, 233
self-discipline, 179
self-discovery, 110
self-esteem, 10, 181, 188, 191
self-improvement, 11, 181, 192, 233
self-realization, 181, 186, 191
    by creating beautiful living space, 10
shame, 71, 178, 192, 218, 233
shapes, 121
    mixing, 15, 27
    of rugs, 90–91
    of sports-related accessories, 122
shelf-scapes, 211
shelving, 68, 114
    open, *18, 26–27, 44, 58, 60, 60–61, 66, 94, 119, 97, 120*
    styling, 35–36, 176
    swing, *228*, 229–31, *229–31*
shopping, 9, 59, 60, 71, 95, 96, 144, 152, 185
side tables, 10, *23, 27, 44, 50, 57, 65, 64, 67, 75, 99, 99, 221*
    bed, 171
    how to make, 220, 222–23, *222–23*
sitting rooms, *40–41*, 42, 44
skateboards, *121*, 128
sliding screen doors, 71
snacks for guests, 140, 155, *155*
social media, 62, 100, 136, 187
sofas, 67, 220
    Art-Deco style, 107
    leather, *23, 26–27, 52, 52, 125*
    moving, 82
    on rugs, 90–91
    placement of, 67, 90–91, 207
    sectionals, 59
    throws on, *19, 23, 39, 40, 50, 57, 65, 69, 91, 105, 107, 125, 160*, 161
    vintage, *26–27*, 27
sofa tables. *See* side tables
softness, 27, 42, 45, 60, 121
solo home, 67, 71, 107
Soria, Catherine (mother of Orlando Soria), 46, 63, 71, 113, 133, 174, 178, 197, 199, 234
Soria, Dale (father of Orlando Soria), 46, 174, 234
Soria, Elisa (sister of Orlando Soria), 115, 234
Soria, Miguel (brother of Orlando Soria), 115, 234

Soria, Orlando, *8, 133, 138, 163*
  apartments, 11, 46, 56, 58, 59, 63, 65, 67, 77, 85, 144, 171, 182
  birth, 9
  blogging, 110, 187, 192
  boyfriends, 5, 11, 58, 62, 67, 99, 107, 165, 170–71, 173, 174, 179, 182
  building DIY projects, *200, 204–5, 208–10, 213–15, 218–19, 223–24, 226–27, 229–31*
  career trajectory, 11, 103, 188, 190–91, 202
  childhood, 9, 46, 48, 55, 59, 115–16, 196–97
  coffee name, 56
  college, 55, 63, 82, 104, 110, 174, 190, 191
  dreams, 20, 22, 31, 48, 55, 56, 232
  family, 111, 113, 114, 156, 185, 190, 196. *See also* Soria, Catherine; Soria, Dale; Soria, Elisa; Soria, Miguel
  friends, 46, 63, 114, 146, 147, 148, 174, 182, 185, 188, 191, 196–99, 223
  gardening, *8, 163, 164*
  in Los Angeles, 22, 24, 46, 48, 63, 65, 140, 188, 190, 223
  in New York, 46, 65, 68, 104, 171, 191
  in Philadelphia, 46
  in Upstate New York, 55
  Orblando, 202, *203,* 204–5, *204–5*
  Orblogdo, 58, 110
  Orcondo, 58, 59, 62
  Orlandiet, 180–81
  parents, 9, 11, 39, 55, 80, 104, 110, 111, 115, 188, 199, 234. *See also* Soria, Catherine; Soria, Dale
  roommates, 68, 170–71, *171, 172,* 173
  siblings, 115, 234. *See also* Soria, Elisa; Soria, Miguel
  teenage years, 9, 45, 122, 191
sound absorbed by rugs, 88
spackle, 83, 85, 87
Spanish Revival home, 46, *47,* 48, *49,* 50, *50–51,* 52, *52,* 53, 95
splurge, 68
stain, 211, 215
staircase, wainscoting on, 42, *43*
stereotypes, 88, 122, 126, 128, 194
Stewart, Martha, 10
straight men, 14, 88, 123, 124, 194
stripes, *43,* 44, *53, 57, 65, 69, 91, 94, 108, 160*
  nautical, 35
  on curtains and drapery, 41, *109*
struggles, 31, 83, 185, 187, 191, 192, 196
  with weight, 62, 179
suburbia, 46, 48–49
success, 105, 191, 196, 233

succulents, planting in containers, 162, *164,* 165–67, *166–67*
surfboards, *121,* 128

T
tablecloths, 151
table linens, 148, 159
tables
  coffee, *19, 32, 39,* 41, 59, *57,* 67, *69,* 90, *106–7,* 128, 158, 159, *207,* 224
    how to make, 206–10, *207–10*
  dining, 15, *20,* 24, *60–61,* 66, 67, 101, 151, *151,* 159, 173, 202, *203,* 224
  glass, *24, 32,* 66, 67, *71, 75*
  round, *27, 43,* 45, *66, 71, 75, 149, 151, 203*
  side, 10, 19, *19, 23, 27, 50, 57, 65, 64, 67, 75,* 99, *125, 221, 225*
    how to make, 220, *222–23, 222–23*
table settings, *149,* 151, *151*
tabletop styling, 159, 211
tansu, 113, *113*
tatami mats, 71
tchotchkes, 60
telescopes, 25, 27
televisions, 44, *126,* 196
  in living rooms, 44, *44*
  in man caves, 123
  lounge, 60
television shows, 29, 31, 41, 100, 188, 192, 202
  Design Star, 191
  Secrets from a Stylist, 202
textiles, hand-dyed, 53, *63*
texting during dinner, 173, *173*
texture, 42, 34, 165, 177
  rug, 88, 90, 121
  wall, 74, 77, 79
therapists, 10, 55
thrift shops, 35, 60, 63, 67, 71, 95, 96, 99, 185. *See also* flea markets
throws, *19, 23, 39, 40, 50, 51,* 53, *53, 57, 65, 69, 91,* 107, 161
tiles, 24
  multi-colored, 20, *20*
  Spanish, 52
toothbrushes, guest, 154, *154*
traditional, 25
  colors, 45
  furnishings, 42, 52
  homes, 59–60
trays, *40,* 44, *52, 98, 105,* 111, *124,* 211, *212*
  how to make, 211, 213–15, *213–15*
  marble/stone, 148
trellis patterns, *50–51,* 52, *53, 64*
trim, in rooms, 59, 60, 74, 76, 77, 79
  white, 45, 77
TVs. *See* televisions

U
upholstered items, 99, 224
  beds, 42, *42,* 60

V
vacuum cleaners, 159, *159*
vases, 132–34, *134,* 207
vintage, 10, 19, 27, 35, 68, 95–96, 99
  accessories, 25
  rugs, 90
  sofa, 27, 107
  store, 67
  vibe, 35

W
wainscoting, 42, *43*
wallpaper, framing, *33,* 35
weddings, 55–56, 193–95
  dresses, 193–94
  music at receptions, 194
  photographs, 111, 114
  presents, 194
weight control, 178–81
weight gain, 62, 162, 179, 187
Weight Watchers, 178
whining, 191, 192
white people, 45, 194
Whole Foods, 152
wicker, 35
windows, 24, 25, 44, 50, 74
window treatments, 20, 59
  hanging curtains, 103, *103*
wine, 147, 148, 186, 199
  rosé, 22, 140, *140,* 147
wood, 126. *See also under* Do It Yourself (DIY) projects: bench; coffee table; side table; swing shelf; tray
  bird candelabra, *94,* 96, 99
  dressers, *81, 96, 98,* 99, *113, 119*
  duck bowl, *96, 96*
  filler, 211, 214, 223
  paneling, 42
  serving planks, 48
wrought iron, 52
  light fixtures, *49, 51*

Y
Yosemite National Park, 9, 46, 104, 115
  Ahwahnee Hotel, 115
  Yosemite Falls, 9, 48
  Yosemite Valley Lodge, 115